MARSHALL EVER AFTER

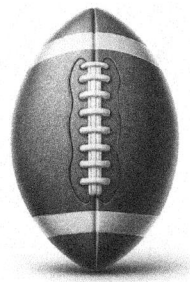

BEYOND THE PLANE CRASH, UNTOLD STORIES

CRAIG T. GREENLEE

ISBN: 978-1-962363-82-2 (sc)
ISBN: 978-1-962363-83-9 (e)

Rev. date: 03/07/2024

CONTENTS

Front cover: Centerpiece photo of 1970 Thundering
Herd football team courtesy of Marshall University

Back cover: Author photo by Cynthia J. Greenlee

To my father, John T. Greenlee, Jr. – Your unwavering support and diverse interests have shaped my world. From sports to symphonies, you opened doors to a rich tapestry of experiences. Our game days and concert nights are cherished memories, and your encouragement ignited my passion for violin and piano. Thank you, Dad, for revealing the multitude of joys life has to offer.

HONORING THOSE WHO PERISHED

November 14, 1970

Coaches
Al Carelli Jr., Jim "Shorty" Moss,
Rick Tolley, Deke Brackett, Frank Loria

Players
Jim Adams, Mark Andrews, Michael Blake, Dennis Blevins,
Willie Bluford, Larry Brown, Thomas Brown, Roger Childers,
Stuart Cottrell, Rick Dardinger, David DeBord, Kevin Gilmore,
David Griffith, Art Harris, Bob Harris, Bobby Hill, Joe Hood,
Tom Howard, Marcel Lajterman, Rick Lech, Barry Nash,
Pat Norrell, Bob Patterson, Scottie Reese, Jack Repasy,
Larry Sanders, Al Saylor, Art Shannon, Ted Shoebridge,
Allen Skeens, Jerry Stainback, Robert VanHorn, Roger Vanover,
Freddy Wilson, John Young, Tom Zborill

Other Staff
Charles Kautz, Gene Morehouse, Jim Schroer,
Donald Tackett, Gary George

Fans
Charles Arnold, Rachel Arnold, Donald Booth,
Dr. Joseph Chambers, Peggy Chambers, Shirley Ann Hagley,
Dr. Ray Hagley, Arthur Harris Sr., Emmett Heath, Elaine Heath,
Cynthia Jarrell, James Jarrell, Kenneth Jones, Jeff Nathan,
Brian O'Connor, Michael Prestera, Dr. Glenn Preston, Phyllis Preston,
Courtney Proctor, Dr. Herbert Proctor, Helen Ralsten,
Murrill Ralsten, Parker Ward, Norman Weichmann

Flight Crew
Captain Frank Abbott, Jerry Smith, Charlene Poat,
Patricia Vaught, Danny Deese

CHERISHED REMEMBRANCE

Paying homage to three contributors to my first memoir (see pages 6, 7, and 8). Their insights, recollections and passion about the Marshall story remain immortalized despite their passing.

Macie Lugo (Passed away December 15, 2017)

A portrait of elegance, Macie epitomized style and class. Her endurance in shouldering profound sorrow over an extended period remains unfathomable. Her willingness to open up about her innermost struggles showcased her grace in confronting life's most painful experiences. Macie's ability to navigate such challenges with fortitude serves as an enduring example to all.

Reggie Oliver (Passed away August 14, 2018)

Reggie stood out as the charismatic force that spearheaded Marshall's football resurgence. Possessing remarkable moxie and game-savvy, "Wolf" admirably steered the Young Thundering Herd in the aftermath of the plane crash. Always gracious in sharing his insights and recollections, Reggie forged a legacy of resilience and an indomitable spirit.

Bill Redd (Passed away June 3, 2022)

My trusted confidant and college roommate. Compassionate, witty and opinionated. Your insightful, on-point recollections were invaluable in helping to make *November Ever After* a memoir worth reading. Bill's legacy lives on and provides lasting evidence that genuine friendships are one of life's greatest treasures.

WHY I WROTE THIS BOOK

Imagine a journey that continues where the heart-stirring tale of *November Ever After* left off. Now, envision a world where *Marshall Ever After* becomes the compass guiding you through even richer narratives, bursting with vibrant details that bring the story to life in a way you've never experienced before.

As the author, I felt compelled to delve deeper into the lives of those who were left behind, their dreams, and their struggles. The need for more vivid narratives was evident. I don't want readers to just observe, but to be intimately engrossed in every emotion, every twist and turn. The pages of *Marshall Ever After* overflow with flavors that tantalize your senses, offering a more profound and captivating reading experience.

But why a second book?

Since the 2011 release of the first book, a continuous flow of new truths, fresh insights, and untold stories have surfaced. This is not merely a rehash; it's a leap beyond. *Marshall Ever After* unveils a treasure trove of revelations, a symphony of untold accounts that paint a more complete picture, addressing the poignant questions left lingering in your mind.

This memoir serves as a bridge between the past and the present, as well as a tribute to those who were left behind in the wake of the Marshall plane crash.

ACKNOWLEDGMENTS

I am forever thankful to the One who is forever faithful – Jesus Christ – the Everlasting One. Thank You Lord for being my provider, my healer, and my waymaker.

My wife Cynthia: As the years go by, my life gets sweeter and sweeter and it's all because of you. Love 'ya much!!

Gregory Dennis: My pastor and trusted friend. Sincerely appreciate you as a man who is true to his calling. You bring the word of God to life everytime you preach. As a result, I am blessed.

Vic Simpson: You have this uncanny knack for producing much-needed materials that help make my job so much easier. Couldn't have completed this project without you.

Lucianne Kautz-Call: An influential force behind the scenes, who combines resourcefulness and enthusiasm to make ideas come to life.

INTRODUCTION

Beneath the bright lights of Joan C. Edwards Stadium, you can feel the electricity. The buzz of the crowd going bananas over Marshall's Thundering Herd. The anticipation in the air hums, punctuated by the sharp crack of helmets colliding with pads. But let's rewind the clock, and let me paint you a different picture.

Before the splendor of "the Joan" with its emerald-green turf, opulent suites, and cutting-edge scoreboard, there stood Fairfield Stadium. It might not have dazzled with grandeur, but it had a certain rugged charm. Patchy grass beneath the players' feet, unyielding seats that held passionate fans, and an undeniably raw atmosphere. Delving into its past, this ambiance made sense; the ground it was built on was once a commercial gravel pit and garbage dump.

Speaking of the stadium turf, have you ever seen a breakaway running back trip over a rogue divot just shy of scoring a touchdown? I have. Football in those days wasn't the glamorous extravaganza that it is now. Yet, it pulsated with an authentic heart and a deep-seated soul. For a brief, golden moment, Marshall teetered on the precipice of greatness. But life, in its ever-twisting narrative, had a different outcome awaiting.

I was there. I breathed the hope, the agony, the resurgence. I remember '68, a year that changed the trajectory of so many lives. A year when young men with stars in their eyes embarked on a journey with the Thundering Herd. Some of them never got to finish that journey. Because of a plane. A crash. A catastrophe that shook a community to its core.

It's unsettling to think I might've been among them, had fate not pulled me in a different direction. My decision to leave the team might've saved my life. And it's a thought that never fades away. It's hard to describe the days after the crash, the pall it cast over everything.

So, why drag these memories up after all this time? Why now?

Because stories like these need to be told. They need to be

remembered. The pain, the despair, and more importantly, the rise from the ashes. It took fourteen years post-crash for Marshall to find its feet again. But boy, when it did, the Thundering Herd was unstoppable.

Fast forward to now, and Marshall is a beacon of progress. We've come a long way since that grim November night, and it's important that the journey isn't forgotten. So, as you dive into these pages, let your heart wander through the shadows of that tragic November evening, but also let it soar with the resurgence that followed. The story you're about to plunge into is raw, poignant, and an absolute emotional rollercoaster.

Welcome, my friend, to *Marshall Ever After*. Keep those tissues close, brace yourself for a ride, and be uplifted by one of the most remarkable comeback stories in sports history.

Forever Remembered: Bronze memorial at Marshall's Joan C. Edwards Stadium honors crash victims. (Photo by Craig T. Greenlee)

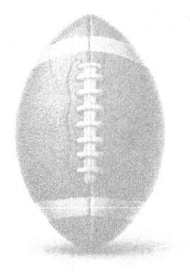

CHAPTER ONE

Days of Yore

Can you imagine the pull of hope and the allure of a dream? That's what beckoned me to the unfamiliar territory of Marshall University back in '68. As a black teen, my roots were deeply embedded in the vibrant rhythms of Jacksonville, Florida. For most of my life, it was the black culture that framed my days and nights. Other than a fleeting summer job here and there, the world outside my culture remained an enigma.

Now, visualize a youthful me, embarking on a journey into Marshall's predominantly white surroundings in Huntington, West Virginia. It was like stepping into a parallel universe! Remember, the late '60s wasn't exactly the poster era for racial harmony, especially in the Deep South. But here's the twist: the electrifying appeal of playing college football had me by the heartstrings. It yanked me right out of my cozy bubble, urging me to chase the horizon.

You see, Jacksonville had its norms. If you were a black high school graduate, you'd probably head off to Florida A&M University or Bethune-Cookman College. But by the spring of my final year at William Raines High School, I was hungry for adventure! The idea of relocating to some distant haven, where the air didn't echo with familiar names, was too tantalizing to resist.

It's worth noting, the late '60s were a tumultuous time. With the Vietnam Conflict in full throttle, college wasn't just an educational institution. For many young men, it was a sanctuary. With the threat of the draft ever-present, attending a college provided a shield from the frontlines of Southeast Asia. And while I was technically "draftable," dodging the army was never my game plan. In my mind, college was my true calling.

Initially, my heart was set on Johnson C. Smith University, a predominantly black school in Charlotte, North Carolina. But life has a way of throwing knuckleballs. Enter Marshall, teasing me with promises of an athletic scholarship throughout summer. But in a plot twist, J.C. Smith left me hanging, no papers to look at, no word on whether I had been accepted or not. That's when the dice rolled in favor of Marshall. Funny thing, most folks back home got it all wrong, thinking I was going to a college in Marshall, Texas. Little did they know, my journey was taking me to a place far more unexpected.

When I mentioned I was heading to West Virginia, the roasts began and never stopped. Seriously, I felt like a marshmallow over a campfire! Given the times, they assumed I'd be the pinch of pepper in a sea of salt. Friends playfully warned, "Get ready to jam with fiddles and banjos!" TV shows like *The Real McCoys* and *The Beverly Hillbillies* didn't help, making everyone think West Virginia was all about hillbilly high jinks. They even dared to predict my new style: "Man, we're gonna see you in white tube socks with dress shoes, and high-water pants with suspenders!!" And here I was, Mr. Fashionista of '68. What had I gotten myself into?

I was flabbergasted to discover that so many people were a little wonky about West Virginia's location. I kid you not, some of those people reckoned it's just a chunk of Virginia that's taken a few steps to the left on the map. They were as far off the mark as a skunk at a perfume convention!

Way back when, around 1863 when Abraham Lincoln was still trying to keep his stovepipe hat in style, West Virginia was indeed a slice of Virginia. But they decided they weren't very comfortable with all the Confederate, pro-slavery hullabaloo. So they packed their stuff, waved arrivederci, and took off faster than a rabbit running from a fox.

Now, I recall some of my friends looking confused when asking me about the mileage between Huntington, West Virginia and Richmond, Virginia. All I could do was chuckle and ask, "Ever checked out an

Atlas?" They treated U.S. geography like it was a game of "Musical Chairs" with the Carolinas or Dakotas.

News flash! West Virginia and Virginia are as different as night and day, like burgers and hot dogs, or Batman and the Joker. Sure, they have some common ground, but they ain't the same. Just like North and South Carolina, or North and South Dakota, they share a smidgen of a name, but not a state line or a Post Office box!

It still amazes me that I ended up at Marshall. Was this a matter of coincidence, or was it destiny? The *day before* I was scheduled to leave home for West Virginia, I received a special delivery package from J.C. Smith with all the paperwork that I should have received weeks earlier. I was relieved that they finally sent me a package. On the other hand, I was miffed that it took so long.

Since I had already purchased my plane ticket and informed Marshall's coaches that I'd come in as a walk-on, my sole focus was getting to West Virginia. This was not a casual journey on a jet. I was on a mission. This was a business trip and I dressed the part: wintergreen sports coat, white dress shirt, necktie, dark trousers, and mahogany dress shoes, complete with a London Fog hat that matched the color of my coat.

On my flight's arrival, the weather was sunny and clear with a few scattered clouds. All I could see from the passenger window were hills and more hills as far as my eyes could see. Geographically, this was so much different from Florida. Huntington is hilly compared to Jacksonville. But the city's terrain is relatively flat when compared to other West Virginia cities, such as Charleston, Bluefield, and Morgantown.

Nothing was going to stop me from earning a roster spot on a college team. Motivation was not a problem, and neither was the possibility that I might get homesick. I dreaded the thought of returning home and having to answer an endless number of questions about why I didn't make it. For me, that would have been the ultimate embarrassment. Somehow, I was going to make the most of this opportunity.

Back then, football was undeniably a second-class sport at Marshall. However, a dramatic metamorphosis began to take place when Perry Moss took over as head coach in '68. At that juncture, Marshall was in freefall as a member of the Mid-American Conference. In the two seasons prior to Moss's arrival, the Herd was woeful at two wins and eighteen losses. Things would not change immediately because NCAA rules prohibited freshmen from playing varsity football and varsity basketball. Marshall went 0–9–1 in Moss's first season, but help was on the way.

Moss's first crop of recruits, the freshman class of '68, was loaded with size, speed, and athleticism. At six feet, 160 pounds, I was not one of those "ripped" individuals. Didn't have much size. What I did have was good hands and better-than-decent giddy up (clocked 4.6 seconds in the forty-yard dash). Plus, I could return kicks and contribute as a wide receiver or defensive back. As for my weight room numbers? Nonexistent. Never lifted weights. Speed and quickness were my fortes and those tools had always served me well. I made the team as a walk-on wide receiver/defensive back. By the time our season began, I was the starter at free safety.

When preseason practice started in early August, more than one hundred players showed up. It was like an NFL training camp. The athletes, many of whom were black, came mostly from the Southern states. Marshall didn't have many black students when the '68 freshman class arrived. The previous year, the school's head count was in the neighborhood of 7,000, which included an estimated 125 blacks. (Documentation of the number of blacks attending MU in '67 is not available.)

In '68, the coaches needed a way to help them sort through all the new faces. We had to put two-inch wide tape on the front of our helmets and write our names on the tape with a felt-tip marker just so the coaches could tell who was who.

Dickie Carter, a sophomore running back that year, has vivid recollections about that first class of recruits brought in by Moss. The varsity occupied one of the practice fields and the freshmen practiced on an adjacent field. Those fields, which were mostly dirt with patches of grass here and there, had no need for manicuring. One of the fields was surrounded by a quarter-mile gravel track. There were days when the combination of dirt, gravel, and swirling winds transformed that field into a veritable dust bowl.

"I remember all the different-colored jerseys," Dickie said. "It seemed like there were enough new players to make two or three teams. And when I looked around and saw so many blacks, it was something that I wasn't used to seeing (at Marshall). After watching the players for a while, I got the feeling that these new guys are gonna be all right."

With so many players coming from so many different places, every freshman had his own narrative to share about coming to West Virginia. The most frequently told story involved a recruit from Louisiana (I can't remember who).

The Greyhound bus creaked to a stop on a steamy day in Bluefield, West Virginia. Dust and the distant sounds of small-town chatter filled the air. As the bus doors swung open, a young stud – thick-set and towering – stepped down onto the curb. He looked around, soaking in the unfamiliar surroundings, then stretched his muscles aching from the long journey. Suddenly, a voice from nearby interrupted his thoughts. "Hey, big guy! Where ya' headed?"

He turned to see an older man, wearing a greasy cap and vest, stuffed with pens and tickets, squinting at him. "Headin' to Marshall," the young man replied, his accent thick with Southern twang. The baggage handler sized him up, the corners of his lips turning into a half- smile. "You one of them football types?"

"Sure am," the young man answered.

Raising an eyebrow, the baggage handler continued. "I dunno son. I heard they've got some beef at Marshall. "How tall are ya?"

The recruit stood a bit taller, pride in his voice. "Six-three."

"How much you weigh?"

"Two-sixty," he replied, puffing his chest out a bit.

The baggage handler took a step back, giving the recruit a long, appraising look from head to toe. After a moment, he nodded, a mischievous grin forming. "Hmmmm. *You just might make it!*"

With so many blacks on Marshall's freshman roster, it was no surprise that prayer became an integral part of the pre-game routine. A vast number of recruits attended all-black high schools in the Deep

South and we were accustomed to praying—as a team—prior to leaving the locker room before the start of every game. Before kickoff in our season opener against the University of Kentucky, the coaches gave their pregame speeches, which stoked our fighting spirit. Then, from somewhere in the back of the locker room, a voice piped up hesitantly. "Hey, ain't we gonna pray or something?"

Silence. Heads turned, eyes scanned, waiting. It felt like one of those scenes from a movie when the music suddenly stops, leaving you on the edge of your seat. Who's gonna lead this? Nobody seemed keen on stepping up. It's weird, you know. In that fleeting moment, I felt this pull. Maybe it was nerves or maybe it was Divine intervention. Without even realizing it, I found myself being the focal point, my voice unsteady, yet genuine. "Lord, just want to thank you for allowing us to be here …"

I was no pastor. I was simply a guy who remembered the prayers from those Sundays during my childhood years in the Episcopal Church. And right then, all I could think of was how lucky I was to be living my dream of playing college football. When I finished praying, the atmosphere had changed. There was this feeling of unity, a newfound sense of purpose. The guys seemed charged and ready. They looked at me with a mixture of surprise and appreciation.

After that day, they never let me forget it. The locker room was always abuzz with shouts of "Hey Preacher!," before every game. Even one of the coaches, a wisecracking graduate assistant, always addressed me as "Rabbi." Who would have ever thought? Me, the team's unofficial prayer leader. Never expected this, but I wasn't complaining.

The influx of new talent produced immediate results and gave hope for a brighter future. Marshall's freshmen went 5–0 and delivered surprising wins over Kentucky and Mid-American Conference powerhouse Ohio University. By mid-October, the freshmen had developed such a high level of confidence that we more than held our own in those Monday scrimmages against the varsity, which Coach Perry Moss often referred to as the "Toilet Bowl." The players moving up to varsity from the unbeaten freshman team were viewed as the saviors-in-waiting for a program that had fallen on hard times.

Talk about swagger. As freshmen, we knew we could handle the varsity because our talent level was so much higher. As it was, competition among the freshmen was so fierce that if you got hurt, you might not get your starting position back. With the rookies getting so much attention, I figured the varsity guys might have some hard feelings. If that was the case, it was never spoken. And besides, why would anyone be envious? Everybody looked forward to the day when Marshall would no longer serve as a bottom-feeder to be pushed around, intimidated, and bullied.

"A football field is the only place in America where you can hit somebody and it's legal."

We heard those words often from freshman coach Pete Kondos, nicknamed "Pistol Pete" by the players. And it became obvious, even to the casual observer, that we took those words to heart. Being physical was the freshman team's hallmark, especially on defense, which had seven blacks in the starting lineup.

Toward the end of the season, we had developed a following. The freshman team got its share of media coverage, not as much as the varsity but more than what most freshman teams usually get. The local newspaper even sent writers on the road to cover our games in person. As for the varsity, it was all downhill (finished 0–9–1 that year). Marshall's frosh drew a decent crowd (around 3,000) for its only home game, which just happened to be our season finale. We won handily over West Virginia Tech in a game that gave the local folks a preview of Marshall's talent level for the next season.

After that final freshman game, we returned to campus. It wasn't long before a dozen youngsters who were at the game stopped by the dorm for a spur-of-the-moment visit. The coaches let us keep our jerseys from that game, but I didn't keep mine for long. One of the kids pleaded non-stop for a souvenir, so I gave him my jersey as a keepsake. I felt like somewhat of a celebrity after that. We had finished the year undefeated and everyone familiar with Marshall was ecstatic about its football future.

The freshman team in '68 was something else! Let me tell you about the three guys who made our days both on and off the field.

First up, there's Robinson Crusoe. Yes, you read correctly. Now, let's be real, when you hear that name, you'd think he was marooned somewhere on an island with only a volleyball for company. But nah, our Crusoe was a wide receiver, and every bit as interesting as his namesake. Straight out of Mobile, Alabama, he had this unique flair about him. You'd always see him in his signature beachcomber attire – those sleeveless tees, those cut-off shorts, and of course, his sandals. I mean, who does that?! Only Crusoe. It's like he always brought a touch of the tropics with him.

Then there was Isaac Tatum. The big man from Louisiana could play linebacker or on the D-line. At first glance, you might wonder what he could bring to the table. He walked a bit funny, all slew-footed. But man, don't be fooled. Tatum was a beast! He was as fast as they came, clocking in at 4.6 seconds in the forty-yard dash! Can you believe that? Watching him play, with his feet pointed outwards, was like seeing a penguin bolt down the field. Such a shame he never got much playing time. We all thought he had a promising future in football, but he opted for the Navy after the first year.

And last but not least, my roommate, Butterball! Oh, I mean Larry Nelson. You wouldn't believe the kind of energy this dude from Pennsylvania brought to the team. Standing at just 5-feet-7 inches and weighing 180 pounds,, he packed a punch at linebacker or running back. I remember that film session of one of our scrimmages when Coach Kondos said he looked like a butterball turkey. We all had a good laugh, but the name stuck. Larry "Butterball" Nelson – that's how we'll always remember him. A stout, solid guy, always ready to "bring it" on the field.

Those three weren't just teammates. They were colorful and memorable and I'm grateful for the memories we shared. Good times, indeed!

The city of Huntington is located in the southwestern part of West Virginia known to many as the Tri-State. The city borders the states of Ohio and Kentucky, and the Ohio River is just a few minutes' drive from campus. It doesn't take long to cross state lines if you're in downtown Huntington. You can still walk or ride a bike across the

6th Street bridge and be in Ohio in a matter of minutes. Or you could drive twenty minutes or so in the opposite direction and find yourself in Kentucky.

Huntington is College Town, USA, and that's not likely to ever change. The city's health-care complex and Marshall's School of Medicine have experienced significant growth. The blue-collar workforce still has a presence but not nearly to the extent of the late '60s. Whether you're in a restaurant or a bank, you can't help but notice the visible reminders (banners, calendars, MU sports photos, and other memorabilia) that validate the city's status as home of the beloved Thundering Herd.

Coming to Huntington in the late '60s was culture shock for me. At that time, Huntington's population was around 70,000, a substantial drop-off from my hometown. Nicknamed the "Gateway City," Jacksonville's population was around 514,000, with blacks comprising about 20 percent of the population. Huntington, by contrast, didn't have nearly as many blacks. I estimate 3,000, maybe 4,000. Back home, I was used to visiting black folks who lived in all four corners of the city and every place in between. In Huntington, you could ride through the black community in twenty to twenty-five minutes.

Being around fewer black folks wasn't the only change I'd have to get accustomed to. I soon discovered that I'd need to make some drastic adjustments in my radio-listening habits. Since Jacksonville had a lot more black folks, it had a couple of black radio stations that played nothing but soul music. By contrast, Huntington was geared more to rock music and country and western. Back home, I was accustomed to listening to The Temptations, James Brown, and Gladys Knight & The Pips on the regular basis. If I was going to listen to music on the radio in West Virginia, I had to get used to a steady diet of Blood, Sweat & Tears, Bob Dylan, and Steppenwolf. Soul music wasn't exactly null and void. Huntington radio stations played rhythm and blues songs every now and then.

For me and the other black students, the only decent source of soul music was located hundreds of miles away in Nashville, Tennessee. We tuned in to WLAC on the AM dial, and we had a jamming good time whenever we could get a strong signal. Listening to WLAC was like being at home. Tuning in to a radio station in Tennessee, though, was a hit or miss proposition. We could get a good signal on clear nights from around eleven o'clock to the wee hours of the early morning. This was far from ideal, but it was better than nothing at all. And it did give me a welcomed break from Engelbert Humperdinck and Johnny Cash.

Getting acclimated to different genres of music was one thing. But it was quite another to learn how the use of one word can produce wildly different responses among people who grew up in different parts of America. When it comes to cultural differences, things aren't always what they appear to be.

Case in point: the use of the word *boy*.

It didn't take long for offensive lineman Ed Carter to learn that a word he perceived to be blatantly offensive, was not a big deal when spoken by somebody from West Virginia. It all started with Ed engaging in a casual conversation with a group of guys during his first year at Marshall. During the discussion, one of the white guys referred to Ed as "boy." The mood turned tense in a hurry, as if a storm had rolled in out of a clear blue sky.

"Until then, I never had any problems with anybody," Ed said. "Where I grew up (in Texas), if somebody called you 'boy,' it was the same as using the n-word. I didn't take too kindly to that, and a friend of mine had to pull me off the guy."

In the aftermath, Ed's friend explained that the word has a much different connotation among West Virginians. It's a common term that's used frequently in everyday conversation."He told me that everybody – blacks and whites – does that in West Virginia. So, then I understood that that's just the way it is."

In the spring of '69, there was an aura of excitement about what was in store for Thundering Herd football. Another batch of blue-chippers and quality walk-ons were headed to Marshall for the upcoming fall season. But little did any of us know that the program would find itself in deep trouble in the coming months. Perry Moss would never get the opportunity to coach his first recruiting class at the varsity level.

That summer, the bottom fell out. An investigation revealed that the school committed more than one hundred recruiting violations, which led to indefinite suspension from the Mid-American Conference and being placed on probation by the National Collegiate Athletic Association. Moss was fired as head coach and reassigned to non-coaching duties. I always thought it was so strange that a coach at a losing program could get busted like that. Usually, schools that break the rules aren't caught for wrongdoing until *after* they've become successful.

My knowledge of the college recruiting process was next to nil. I didn't get much playing time as a back-up quarterback in my senior year of high school. So, I was really an unknown commodity. I never had any phone conversations with college coaches. Recruiters never made any visits to the Greenlee household. I didn't need to be a Rhodes Scholar to figure out that a position switch was in order. In those days, playing quarterback at a white school in the South was not a viable option for the black athlete. My best shot at making the grade at Marshall would be as a pass catcher or pass defender.

The fact that I attracted some interest as a back-up quarterback was not all that surprising. It's not like I was some marginal scrub sitting at the end of the bench. As a high school senior, I was the starting quarterback until a knee injury suffered a week before the season opener caused me to miss six games.

Unbeknownst to me at the time, Marshall engaged in a massive letter-writing campaign to high school football coaches all across the South. Coach Perry Moss wanted to bring in as many players as possible and he didn't care about skin color. Since MU was a perennial loser, Moss searched far and wide for talent that could deliver an immediate turnabout. Marshall sent letters to some of my high school teammates and a few guys I played against. As things turned out, though, I was the only player from Jacksonville to cast my lot with the Thundering Herd that year. I knew it was a risk to travel so far from home to a school I had no familiarity with whatsoever. To me, the risk was worth it.

Marshall University
Football Office
Huntington, West Virginia 25715

                    MR. CRAIG GREENLEE
                    5908 LUSAID DR.
                    JACKSONVILLE, FLA. 32209

        Thought for the week —

        "Two men looked out from prison bars —
        One saw mud, the other stars."

As a high school senior in '68, Marshall University's football office sent me weekly postcards, which further stoked my passion for the game.

Marshall's freshman football team of '68 fared so well that fan interest soared to unprecedented levels. Expectations were so high that it was inevitable that at some point somebody, somewhere, would raise enough questions to trigger an investigation. How was it that a perennial loser was able to suddenly attract so many top-grade athletes? If Moss's first recruiting class was a sign of things to come, it wouldn't take long for the Herd to go from being a weak link to being a genuine powerhouse.

It was common knowledge in '68 that certain players got cash payments and special favors. All this came to light when one of the pay-for-play athletes decided to quit going to spring practice. The player was informed that his payments would cease if he didn't return. The player, whose identity has never been revealed publicly, told a relative about his situation. This relative, who had strong connections with another school in the MAC, contacted the conference and shared with them what he had learned. It was only a matter of months before the league gave Marshall the boot.

Players getting paid in dollars and favors were not the only misdeeds. The program was also plagued by irregularities involving financial aid and federally insured student loans. My experience with favors and money was zero. I never got free dry cleaning and never received any unmarked envelopes with $100 to $200 cash inside, which I'm told was the standard pay in those days. What I do know about is the loan I assumed as a freshman.

During preseason camp, a day was set aside for most of the freshmen to go downtown to one of the banks. I can't remember exactly how many of us went, but it was quite a few, including my two roommates. There were enough of us in the building that it resembled a Friday afternoon when banks are crowded with people standing in line to cash their paychecks. As far as I know, most of us got $1,500 loans. As for how the money was spent, I don't remember spending much on school-related items unless it was something like notebooks, pens, and pencils. I do not recall making any payments for tuition, room and board, or books. As far as I was concerned, the loan was really spending money, which I used mostly to buy clothes, record albums, and off-campus meals.

With all the talent Perry Moss assembled that first year, it still causes me to wonder about the what-ifs.

- What would have happened if everybody on that freshman team had stayed?

- What would have happened if there had been no recruiting scandal and Moss had kept his job?
- How much further along would the program be if Moss could have added other recruiting classes to further enhance an already talent-rich pool of players?
- How would things have turned out if the plane crash had never happened?

Given the Herd's dismal varsity record from '65 through '68, the success of the '68 freshman team guaranteed that wholesale personnel changes were imminent. Upperclassmen, for the most part, did not figure prominently in Moss's game plan. The annual varsity-alumni game of '69 provided clear confirmation of the much-anticipated overhaul. Nineteen of the starting twenty-two players on offense and defense came from that undefeated freshman team.

With so many newcomers named as starters, it seemed like this could be the start of a wonderful winning tradition. If this group remained intact, Marshall had the makings of what could have been a super team by the time the freshmen reached their senior season. And just maybe we would have been good enough to win the MAC and get an invite to the Tangerine Bowl. That would have been a special treat for me, since that bowl game was played in Orlando, Florida, which was roughly a three-hour drive from my home in Jacksonville.

Prior to the start of spring practice that year, there was potential for trouble on the horizon. Most of the black freshmen were not happy about the scholarship situation. We came to Marshall with the explicit promise that we would earn a scholarship when we made the team. That had not happened by the start of the spring semester, so there was talk about boycotting spring practice as a means to get that matter settled.

In our minds, we had sufficient leverage to help us get what we wanted. After all, we were the catalysts that would spark much-needed change for a floundering program. As a team, we had every reason to believe that the best was still yet to come. It was clear that black athletes would get substantial playing time under Moss. Marshall needed better athletes to compete and win. In this case, most of the top players coming in happened to be black.

Staging a boycott was not a matter of the players simply paying lip service to the idea. After much discussion, we decided against it. Instead, we opted to let our play on the field do our talking for us. In the end, things worked out for our best interests. We got those scholarships.

All of us were sold on Coach Moss's ambitious plan to upgrade MU football. And we were certain that it wouldn't take that long. Attracting enough football talent would not be an issue – the '68 freshmen team was proof of that. A fairly quick turnaround would have been quite a coup, when you consider the state of Marshall University athletics when Moss arrived on the scene in January '68. Football seemed to fill that role as an unwanted stepchild.

In contrast, basketball was the centerpiece of the school's sports universe. The Thundering Herd routinely attracted its share of top-rated recruits, which included a few high school All-Americans. Memorial Field House, the school's home arena, was filled close to capacity most of the time. Fan interest was intense. During those golden days, Marshall was on fire. The Herd danced its way to the National Invitational Tournament, not once but twice in a row, even shimmying its way to the semifinals one magical year. Back in the day, getting to the NIT was the Mount Everest that every team aimed to climb.

As the '70s rolled in, enter stage right: Mike D'Antoni, a wizard of a point guard in his second year at MU. Dude was smooth. Post-college, he took his talents to the National Basketball Association and Italy. But like a boomerang, he returned to America and made waves as a head coach. D'Antoni wasn't just any coach. He was an offensive mastermind with the Phoenix Suns, Los Angeles Lakers, New York Knicks and Houston Rockets. But here's a fun fact: even though D'Antoni had much dazzle in his game, he was not *the man* at Marshall.

It was Russell Lee, a supremely-gifted forward who closed out his college career as an All-American in 1972. The Herd finished the season ranked twelfth nationally in the final polls. Russell, six feet, five inches tall, was the No. 1 draft pick of the Milwaukee Bucks in the 1972 NBA draft. The Bucks, who had won the NBA championship the previous season with Kareem Abdul-Jabbar and Oscar Robertson, were so impressed with Russell that they picked him ahead of their other first-round pick: a guy named Julius Erving from the University of Massachusetts. "Dr. J" never suited up for the Bucks. Instead, he started his Hall of Fame career with the Virginia Squires of the American Basketball Association.

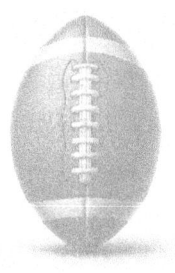

CHAPTER TWO

A Time of Testing

I spent the whole time at home during the summer of '69. This was the close-out year of a topsy-turvy decade, and the late '60s were especially turbulent. The assassinations of Dr. Martin Luther King Jr. and Bobby Kennedy produced widespread feelings of despair which cut across all color lines. The escalation of the Vietnam Conflict and the increased frequency of war protests on college campuses dominated newspaper headlines and television newscasts.

The struggle for civil rights continued, but the popular sentiment among the black masses started to change to some extent. "Say loud, I'm black and I'm proud" was just as much of a catchy mantra as "we shall overcome." In the meantime, the women's movement gained added momentum by shining the spotlight on gender inequality. The hippies and their accompanying drug culture were fixtures on the American landscape. With so much going on in society, you couldn't help but be aware. For me, however, football was still the centerpiece of my existence.

When August rolled around,, I was excited and anxious to get back to campus for the start of preseason practice. After my arrival, the familiar sights and sounds of Marshall were supposed to be comforting, but something felt off. Since I had not kept tabs on the goings-on in Huntington, I was shocked to hear about the Herd being put on NCAA probation and kicked out of the Mid-American Conference.

Frantic to get more info, I checked into my dorm, left my bags unpacked, then high-tailed it to the football office. To my surprise, it wasn't the usual hub of activity. Instead, the atmosphere was somber, and the halls echoed a bit too loudly.

And then I saw Pete Kondos, alone in his office, packing up all of his belongings. Not sure what I should say, all I could come up with was "Hey Coach." Kondos, my freshman coach and newly-promoted varsity defensive coordinator, greeted me with a worn and weary look in his eyes. Without prompting, he began to fill in the gaps – Kondos and Perry Moss lost their jobs, the program was on probation, and quite a few teammates transferred. It was a lot to process. The Marshall I knew, the team and the dream I committed to, now seemed to be falling apart right in front of me. After sharing the grim details, he stretched out his hand in a gesture of camaraderie. "Wish you the best, Craig. You're a good football player."

With those words, Kondos departed, leaving me standing in the dimly-lit hallway, grappling with the new reality for my team and the uncertain path that lay ahead.

The severity of Marshall's transgressions had serious repercussions. The Thundering Herd's roster shrank dramatically. For spring ball, there were eighty-three players on hand. When fall practice started, the varsity had only forty-one players. It was a substantial drop-off in manpower. In spite of the mass exodus, there were others, like myself, who decided to stay. Since I was on scholarship and in the starting lineup, there was no compelling reason for me to leave. Based on all the dramatic changes that took place in such a short period of time, those of us who returned should have sensed that the upcoming season would be radically different from what we experienced as freshmen.

One of the most critical losses was Ron Mickolajczyk, an offensive tackle from New Jersey. In my eyes, Mickolajczyk (pronounced MICK-o-LANjik) was a vastly different breed of athlete. "Mick" was six feet, three inches, 250 pounds, and all muscle. One of the local sportswriters tabbed him as "Hercules."

I had never seen a guy that big who walked on his toes. Maybe that explains why he consistently ran 4.8 seconds in the forty-yard dash, a cheetah-swift clocking for an offensive lineman. "Mick" came back for preseason practice but stayed just two days before transferring to the University of Tampa, where he became a three-year starter. Ron played two seasons with the Toronto Argonauts of the Canadian Football League and then played four more seasons with the New York Giants.

The timing of Moss's firing forced school officials to move quickly to fill that vacancy. Two days before the start of preseason practice, Rick Tolley was named as the interim coach. Tolley himself was still new to MU at the time. He joined Moss's staff as a defensive line coach in the spring of '69. Most of the players didn't know much about him, other than he had been an assistant at Ferrum Junior College (Virginia) in '65 when the Panthers won their first junior college national championship.

What I remember most about Coach Tolley from that spring was how hard he worked the defensive linemen. Every time I looked around, I'd hear those guys wheezing and gasping for air as they finished running forty-yard dashes. Little did the rest of us know that we'd get a lot of the same in the weeks to come after Tolley was given the reins to run the team. Rick Tolley was not one of those drill-sergeant types. Getting in your face, nose-to-nose was not his style. He had a quiet, but fierce demeanor about him. You *knew* that he did not play games, he had no favorites, and he worked everybody—*hard*. By any and all standards, he was a tough taskmaster. Tolley made sure that conditioning was never an issue. We were always running wind sprints.

Even with Perry Moss and some key players from the freshman team no longer onboard, the '69 version of the Herd was still much better than the varsity from the year before. But it would take a while before the Marshall faithful could bask in the glow of watching their team win a few games by season's end.

The year of '69 was college football's centennial. The first college game ever played was between Rutgers and Princeton in November 1869. To commemorate the occasion, the National Collegiate Athletic Association distributed football-shaped decals nationwide for college teams to put on their helmets. The multicolored decal was blue with red trim, and the number "100" (in white type) was framed by a football.

Players on every team also received a certificate acknowledging their participation in college football's one-hundredth season.

The team's headgear for that season was hopelessly vanilla in my opinion. Instead of a school insignia, jersey number, or mascot—artwork that typically appeared on the side of the helmet—the only graphics placed on Marshall's milky-white helmets were those centennial decals and jersey numbers in small type on the back of the helmet.

MU's Deep Defenders Among Best Sophs in Country—Tolley

By LOWELL CADE
Advertiser Sports Writer

Pass defense hasn't been one of Marshall's strong suits in football over the years, and especially during the past two.

And, this year it looks like Coach Rick Tolley will intrust the responsibility to three sophomores — Larry Sanders, Craig Greenlee and Nathanial (Nat) Ruffin. But don't sell this trio short.

"I'd stack them up against the best sophomores in major college football," said Tolley this week.

Last year the MU secondary was fifth among Mid-American Conference teams in pass defense, giving up an average of 127 yards per game, and nine touchdowns. The Herd defenders picked off 11 enemy aerials. Graduated Joe Ralbusky and departed Mike Smith led the way in numbers with three apiece.

10 Interceptions

In five freshmen games last year, the Little Herd pass defenders picked off 10 enemy aerials, and Greenlee led the pack with four.

Greenlee's a 6-0, 166-pounder from Jacksonville, Fla. Ruffin is 5-11, 176 from Quincy, Fla., and Sanders, 6-1, 195, is from Tuscaloosa, Ala.

All are versatile performers. Due to a recent outbreak of minor injuries on the offense to receivers, Tolley has had to press all three into service as backup duty at flanker and split end.

Tolley says he feels Ohio State couldn't have three better sophomores on the field. "I know there are better veteran defensive backs," he said. "Experience means a lot. But these sophomores have good speed, range and are good tackles. In short, they have a lot of potential. But, they're sophomores and they're apt to make sophomore mistakes."

* * *

Thursday the Herd, even the coaches, welcomed the end of two-a-day drills. Classes begin Monday and practice time has been set for 3 p.m. Saturday even the Herd will work out at Fairfield Stadium before only Big Green Club members and faculty. Today's one workout was also set for 3 o'clock.

The coaches made one line-up change Thursday when sophomore Willie Bluford was promoted to No. 1 fullback ahead of junior Dick Carter.

"He's one of the most improved players we have," said Tolley. "He looks faster than he did last spring, he's making fewer mistakes, running hard and blocking well. On top of that he's a great kid with a fine attitude."

CRAIG GREENLEE
Sophomore safety

In '69, Marshall's all-sophomore secondary had fans buzzing with anticipation after their undefeated freshman season in '68.

In the '69 season opener, Marshall's sophomore-dominated squad played like rookies in a 27–14 road loss at Morehead State University (Kentucky). For the sophomores, it was our first varsity game—and it showed. There were a plethora of mistakes on both sides of the football that night. The Herd was flagged for 180 yards in penalties.

Some news accounts of that game zeroed in on Marshall's young secondary getting torched for 243 yards and four touchdowns. A large chunk of that yardage came on short check-off passes to the running back in the flat, which was a "soft spot" in our zone defense. We never made the adjustment defensively and Morehead State took full advantage all game long.

I did come up with one drive-killing interception in the second half: a midair take-away that turned out to be the first and only interception of my college career. In the fourth quarter, I added to our mountain of miscues when I attempted to get a quick jump on a pass to the flat. In my eagerness to make a play, I left my area of the field open. My mental lapse resulted in blown coverage and the Eagles scored the go-ahead touchdown.

It was bad enough that we didn't play up to our capabilities against Morehead State. But even worse was that we had practice on a Sunday afternoon after playing a game on Saturday night. I wasn't sure what to expect. We went through our usual warm-ups and drills and it appeared that we would head to the showers after about forty-five minutes on the field, which turned out to be wishful thinking.

Before leaving the field, all the players were divided into groups according to position and we started running forty-yard dashes. We lined up and broke into a sprint when Tolley blew his whistle. Then we'd turn around, line up again and take off at the sound of another whistle. Back and forth we went. We were not allowed to rest between sprints. It still boggles my mind that we ran so much *the day after* playing a game.

As we continued to run, I looked around and saw that we had attracted a small audience. I saw ten, maybe fifteen, students who lived in the dormitory located across the street from the practice field watching us from their rooms. When we finally finished, all the players were dog-tired. We ran *forty-four* all-out forty-yard dashes—that's a mile's worth! Forty-four was the official count, according to Bill Redd, a fellow student and friend of mine. Bill, who was not an athlete, never explained why he started keeping count. Guess he had a feeling that after losing to Morehead State the way we did that we'd probably get some extra work when we went to practice.

There was a lot more agony than ecstasy for most of the '69 season. By late October, we were 0–6. In the meantime, Marshall had a twenty-seven-game losing streak dating back two seasons and was on the verge of setting a new NCAA record for consecutive losses.

As players, we realized that like it or not, Herd football was synonymous with losing. I remember several instances that provided indisputable evidence of that ugly truth. On road trips, we'd frequently see homecoming queens and floats when our team bus arrived at the stadium. Teams do not schedule their toughest opponents for homecoming. Of all games, nobody wants to lose at homecoming and spoil the festive atmosphere of the celebration. Given those facts of life, it's no wonder that Marshall seemed to be just about everybody's opponent of choice for their homecoming games.

We should have beat Morehead State in the opener, but we didn't. We came tantalizingly close to beating Northern Illinois, but ended up losing 18–17 on a late field goal. The rest of the games up to that point in the season—Toledo, Miami (Ohio), Western Michigan, and Louisville—ended as predicted with lopsided losses. With four games left to play, team morale wasn't exactly soaring. The way things had been going, the possibility that we might finish the season winless seemed very real.

The most physically painful loss came against the University of Toledo. Toledo is my birthplace, and one of my uncles lived there. I never knew much about the city because I only lived there a couple of years before moving to Florida. In every sense, the Toledo game was a game of hard knocks. The Rockets had this beefy bruiser of a fullback: Charles Cole. He's what I call one of those wide-load runners at 230-plus pounds. On one play, Cole broke free at the line of scrimmage and headed toward the sideline.

As a defensive back, you like it when a big back decides he can outrun you to the corner. A smaller, faster defender has an easier time of going low and taking a big man's legs away from him. That's how I was taught to tackle when I started to play the game. *The bigger they come, the harder they fall.* That was the mantra we used during my sandlot football days as a youngster.

But this time, I forgot all about what worked on the playground and I went after the big fella. Cole turned upfield and we had a head-on collision. I hit him chest high, linebacker-style, and took him down. What happened next was a telltale sign of who got the best of it. Cole sprung to his feet quickly. So did I, but I didn't walk away like I was ready for more. Stunned by this stabbing pain, I felt like I had been smacked in the neck with a two-by-four. I found out later that it was a pinched nerve, a nagging injury that players learn to live with.

When I came off the field, the pain was so excruciating that I took my helmet off. I wasn't aware of it at the time, but a school newspaper photographer zeroed in on my bout with agony and the snapshot he took ran in *The Parthenon*. The photo caption referred to Marshall's agony of defeat. Losing had nothing to do with that particular moment. Intense pain had everything to do with it. It took nearly two years *after* I quit playing football for the pain in my neck to finally stop.

I was my own worst enemy that season. Lack of consistency prevented me from getting more playing time. I'd start one game, play poorly, and then sit the bench for a few games. At midseason, I turned in one of my better performances in a 48–14 blowout loss at Western Michigan University. I didn't start but played the entire second half and finished with eight solo tackles. That's a lot for someone who plays safety, a position that's the last line of defense.

Marshall's defensive backs were very busy that day. Starting cornerbacks Larry Sanders and Nate Ruffin played the whole game and ended up with fifteen unassisted tackles apiece. The fact that our secondary was in so many tackles was a clear indication of how badly we were mauled at the line of scrimmage.

Next on the schedule was a road game at the University of Louisville, and I was back in the starting lineup. Lee Corso, a longtime college football analyst on the ESPN television network, was the Cardinals coach at the time. My status as a starter, however, was short-lived. The Louisville game turned out to be the absolute lowest moment for me as an athlete. The third quarter wasn't even halfway over before I lost my starting position *again*, and I had no one to blame but myself.

It's a play I'll never forget. Louisville running back Jim King caught a pass from Gary Inman coming out of the backfield. As I came up to make the hit, I had a flashback from the Toledo game when I injured my neck after making a tackle. I was unable to block out the memory of the pain I suffered from that hit, and I didn't want to relive that moment again.

King wasn't nearly as hulky (around 195 pounds) as Toledo's beastly fullback, but the memory from that collision in the TU game would not go away. I was not at full speed when I made contact, so I wasn't able to deliver enough of a blow to take him down. It was a weak effort on my part, and King bowled me over around the thirteen-yard line on his way to a thirty-four-yard touchdown. It came as no surprise when I was banished to the bench for the rest of the night. Marshall lost 34–17. It was a long and lonely bus ride back to West Virginia. Yes, I was embarrassed. But eventually I got over it.

Ironically, it was Marshall's homecoming that set the tone for a desperately needed turnaround. On paper, it didn't seem remotely possible that the Herd had any chance of pulling off a shocking upset of Bowling Green State University. History favored the Falcons, who had not lost to Marshall in fourteen years. The seeds for surprise were sown in the days leading up to the homecoming game. The slogan for week—"Stop the streak"—captured the imagination of students and townspeople alike. For the first time in a long time, there was genuine excitement about the possibility that the Thundering Herd would actually win a game for the first time in more than two seasons.

The anticipation of victory was evident in every practice that week. Everybody was tuned in to having good practices during the week, which typically leads to playing well on Saturdays. The dorms and many of the fraternity and sorority houses were adorned with signs of encouragement for the Herd to whip the Falcons. Late in the week, a bonfire pep rally was held at the intramural field located near the center of the campus. A crowd of around 500 people showed up for the event.

The game itself was fun to watch, even though I didn't get to play one down—not even on kickoffs or punt coverage. Our defense allowed over 400 yards but delivered when it really mattered with two interceptions and five forced fumbles. In the cold, wetness, and mud, Marshall pounded its way to a 21–16 upset win. In spite of the slosh, puddles, and potholes, fans swarmed the grounds at Fairfield Stadium to congratulate the players.

Weather conditions for Homecoming '69 made it easy to determine who played and who didn't. Since I sat on the bench for the whole game, my uniform was spotless, except for my cleats, which were packed with mud from taking part in warm-ups. After the game, I took some good-natured ribbing about not getting any playing time, but I didn't care.

Well, that's what I told myself.

One of my buddies, always the comedian, suggested that I should have dived on the ground and muddied myself to give the appearance that I had played. "Hey, maybe then people would think you actually stepped onto the field!" he teased. But that was never going to happen. I had way too much pride for that; I didn't see any use in trying to fake people out. Even though I didn't play, I was thrilled that we finally got that long-awaited breakthrough. We avoided the distinction of being the team that led the nation in losing.

As things turned out, the Bowling Green victory set the stage for a magnificent run in which Marshall closed out the season by winning three of its last four games.

After seeing little or no game action for three consecutive weeks, I was ready to get back on the field for the season finale against Mid-American Conference title contender Ohio University. I didn't start, but did get some meaningful minutes, mostly on passing downs.

This game had a memorable ending. Down 24–7 at halftime, Marshall roared back to take a 35–31 lead with a little over a minute left to play in the contest. Ohio put together a frantic final drive and had the ball inside the Herd's five-yard line. It was a goal-line situation and I was pulled out of the game and replaced by starting safety Kevin Gilmore.

Watching from the sideline, I had a gut feeling the next play would be a pass to the tight end. I kept repeating: "Watch the tight end! Watch the tight end!" Perhaps nobody thought I knew what I was talking about. As a former quarterback, I was certain it was the right play to call. Running the ball was the safe approach for short yardage, so a pass play would most likely catch the defense by surprise.

Sure enough, Ohio quarterback Steve Skiver took the snap and fired a quick pass to the tight end on the right side. The usually sure-handed Gilmore was in position to make the game-saving interception near the goal line, but the pass ricocheted off his chest and fell to the turf. The Bobcats still had enough time to run another play, and they scored with five seconds remaining on Paul Kapostasy's short plunge. Ohio University escaped with a 38–35 victory.

The game's closing moments provided great theater for the fans. For the losing team, the aftertaste of defeat was comparable to sucking a barrelful of lemons. Two highly questionable pass interference calls on Nate Ruffin on that final drive literally gave the game to Ohio on a platinum platter.

It's interesting to speculate, but the bottom line is that no human being will ever know what would have happened had I stayed in the game. It's not that Kevin had bad hands. He played running back and tight end before being switched to defense. Who knows? Maybe I would have missed the interception too. But usually you come up with the interception when you know who the quarterback is looking to throw to. And I knew where the ball was going. I expected it. Just call this another case of the what-ifs.

Sometimes I think that had I been on the field and made the interception, it might have caused me to change my mind about quitting the game. Had that occurred, it's quite possible that I would have played ball the following season.

For me, October '69 was a pivotal time. Football had become a see-saw proposition with a lot more downs than ups. What it really came down to was whether I really wanted to continue playing this game. At one point earlier in the season, I became so despondent that I purposely missed a few practices and seriously considered putting the pads away for good. I dreaded going to practice. I didn't want to put in the necessary time to make myself a better player. The desire wasn't there anymore. There was no way I could fake it. Nobody pressured me one way or the other in my decision-making. In the final analysis, I opted to return for the remainder of the season. In doing so, I could honestly say to myself that I finished what I started.

I don't recall exactly at what point in October that I reached a decision about the '69 season being my last. I played in six games and started three times that year.

Even though the Ohio game was my *last hurrah,* my love for the sport had not diminished. Still, I was keenly aware that the searing passion to compete was noticeably absent. Without that gnawing hunger to push me, there would be no full commitment, and that just wasn't good enough. At that juncture, I figured it was best for me to focus my energies on improving my grades and graduating.

My college football career wasn't what I hoped it would be. And I have to admit that I rarely agreed with my position coach when I played varsity ball in '69. Frank Loria coached the defensive backs and he relentlessly bombarded our psyche with one message: *"If you do the little things, the big things will come."*

Loria was a two-time All-America safety at Virginia Tech University in '66 and '67. He played in the same secondary with longtime Virginia Tech coach Frank Beamer. Loria was as close to being a contemporary of ours as anyone on the coaching staff. When Tolley brought Loria onboard, he hadn't been out of college for that long, which meant he wasn't that much older than any of the players. Coach Loria and I didn't see eye to eye, but he was *on point* about that constant message that none of the defensive backs would ever forget. In my career as a journalist, I've learned that paying attention to detail, learning your craft, and proper preparation make a world of difference. It's often the difference that separates the average from the excellent.

My days as a Marshall athlete also provided opportunities for me to learn how to constructively deal with frustration and failure. To overcome adversity, it's necessary to work through difficulties while maintaining the confidence to know within yourself that success is achievable. Most of all, you should never be satisfied with the status quo if your goal is to improve your current status.

Tackling was the major issue I had with Coach Loria. Defensive backs weighing 160 pounds like me generally had a tough time taking down 230-pounders the way he wanted it done. Loria loved that textbook-style hit where the defender launches head first into the runner's chest and then drives the runner to the turf. Coach demonstrated the technique in practice but followed up by showing us how he did it when he played in college.

The film clip we watched often was from a game between Syracuse University and Virginia Tech. Jim Nance, the bull elephant fullback from Syracuse, took a handoff inside the five-yard line and was headed to the end zone. Loria, who was five feet, nine inches, 175 pounds, met Nance head-on and stopped him cold for no gain.

Couldn't argue with what I saw on the film. It just went against everything I'd ever been taught when I learned to play the game on the playground. I was always the youngest player on the field playing against kids who were three to four years older. They always told me: *"I don't care how big a man is. If you take away the legs, he's going down."*

I never embraced Coach Loria's way of tackling, but there was no way for me to avoid it. Every day in practice, we'd have head-on tackling. I will say one thing for those drills: all that heavy hitting really developed the neck area. I had one of those football bull necks and didn't really notice it until I went home for the holidays when everybody kept talking about it.

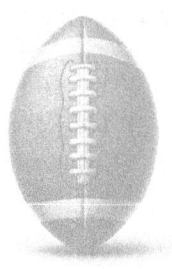

CHAPTER THREE

The Cold Embrace of Bias

There weren't any racial tensions on Marshall's football team in '69. Blacks and whites got along just fine. But away from the games, practices, team meetings, and study halls, it was a much different scenario.

At best, socializing among the black and white players was minimal. You wouldn't see any black players going to any parties hosted by the white fraternities and white sororities. Likewise, you'd never see any white guys showing up at a hotel or house party hosted by black folks. And it didn't matter if the party's location was near campus or in the heart of "the hood." That's just the way it was. Blacks and whites seemed to be comfortable with that. Nobody felt the need to come out of their cultural comfort zone. Of course there were a few blacks and whites who intermingled frequently, but it wasn't commonplace. After all, this was Huntington, not Greenwich Village in New York or somewhere on the West Coast.

The late '60s marked the arrival of the first wave of black athletes coming to Marshall, which before then didn't have many black students. At this juncture, the school started to actively recruit more blacks for football and basketball.

At the same time, there was another movement taking place not only at Marshall, but at other colleges around the South. Up until then, it was standard procedure for black folks to attend historically black institutions. But even that was starting to change as a greater number of blacks who were not athletes opted to enroll in predominantly white schools. This trend was set in motion, in large part, by the desegregation of the public school systems in the Deep South. With more blacks attending mainstream schools, there was bound to be some uneasiness among the races. There were a lot of whites who had never been around black people before, and vice versa. So it was inevitable that, at some point, there would be incidents that would spark racial unrest.

Macie Lugo encountered racial bigotry at Marshall while moving into her assigned dorm room in August '69. Classes had not even started yet. Macie, a freshman, was exhausted because her arrival was delayed after the station wagon she was riding in broke down and needed to be repaired. It took several hours for the repairs to be completed. It wasn't until after ten o'clock at night that she finally reached her destination.

Macie got off the elevator on her floor with two friends carrying her luggage. As they walked down the hall looking for her room, they noticed two white students coming from the opposite direction. As they approached Macie and her companions, they started to talk loudly— apparently on purpose—so that Macie could hear the conversation.

"I bet you that's your roommate," the first girl said.

"If it is my roommate," the second girl responded, *"then I'm moving out."*

Sure enough, the white girl moved out just as she promised.

"That," said Macie, "was my introduction to Marshall University."

*****

As a wide-eyed freshman, I dove right into college life at Marshall, ready for new experiences. But, oh boy, did I get a rude awakening about the vibe there. It was as if the campus atmosphere mirrored the town's overall feel. The real eye-opener, though? It came in the last place I expected – a church.

So here's the deal: Back home (Jacksonville, Florida), I was kind of the odd one out. Not because I had any quirky habits, but because I was this black guy attending an Episcopal Church. Most of the black folks I knew were Baptist, Methodist, African-Methodist-Episcopal, or Holiness. As for Jacksonville? It had only two all-black Episcopal churches. So, piecing it all together, I figured the Episcopal scene in the smaller town of Huntington would more than likely be all-white.

But, to be honest, that didn't faze me. I just wanted what was familiar, the faith I'd grown up with. Change? Nah, wasn't in the mood for that. So, one Sunday, I decided to take a twenty-minute stroll from my dorm to this Episcopal church nearby.

Here's where things got interesting.

As soon as I stepped in, boom! It hit me. I was the only black person in the room. If those faces could talk, oh, the tales they'd spin that day. Most people looked, well, shocked. Like my mere presence was ... weird or something, like I was an intruder. The pastor? He was like, "Hey, welcome! How are you?" But the others? Cold vibes all around.

That experience got my mind racing. See, in my church back home, when we have Holy Communion, everyone walks to the altar, kneels, and yeah, we all share wine from the same cup. But given those odd stares I got, I couldn't help but wonder, would anyone hesitate to sip after me? It really made me question – were these folks truly genuine in their faith?

Despite the pastor's good intentions, that place just didn't resonate with me. So, I decided it wasn't my scene and never went back.

*****

In the late '60s, college campuses all across the country served as forums for public demonstrations, and Marshall University was no different. The fall semester of '69 provided an unexpected opportunity for Marshall's black athletes to actively engage in peaceful dissent.

Here's the story:

School administrators promised to give Black United Students office space in the Student Union building. BUS, a campus organization, needed a base of operations. Weeks and months passed and BUS, which had about one hundred members, was still without a home. The administration's promises had not been kept, which gave the clear impression that the school wasn't serious about delivering on its promise.

The formation of the Student Relations Center as the home for

BUS would satisfy several needs and would be open to students of all cultures and racial backgrounds. The Center would do the following:

- Serve as a focal point for the cultural, social, and intellectual interests of black students;
- Be an on-campus agency to promote racial understanding;
- Fill that role as a university agency to handle charges of discrimination involving students and campus entities.

In response to the administration's lengthy delay in providing office space, the BUS leadership came up with the idea to stage a protest at the president's convocation, an event in which the school's president discussed the state of affairs of the university. Bob Wright, John Shellcroft, Howard Henderson, Diane Pegram, Lee Ernest McClinton, Don Ross, and Bill Dodson were the student activists who helped develop the BUS strategy to effectively voice our concerns.

The demonstration had its disappointing aspects. BUS didn't get nearly as much support from black athletes as expected. In all, maybe ten black jocks (football and basketball players) participated. Many were reluctant to publicly support the protest. They didn't want to be connected with any activity that would be viewed as controversial. Back then, black people who engaged in demonstrations were often referred to as "black militants," which had negative connotations. It was a term most closely associated with organizations such as the Black Panthers, which in those days was considered to be a subversive group by the federal government. Nobody I talked to ever admitted this, but it was said that some of the black athletes feared they might lose their scholarships if they protested.

For those of us who believed in engaging in peaceful dissent, this was not a time to sit down and keep quiet. Yes, playing ball on scholarship was our means to pay for our college education. But we were students too. And we saw no valid reason why black students shouldn't have access to the same resources, programs, and opportunities that other campus organizations had access to.

The demonstration was scheduled for Thursday in the early afternoon and the timing couldn't have been better. For the football players who wanted to participate, it meant that we had ample time to protest and still get to practice on time. About seventy-five black students arrived early at the scene of the President's Convocation. We sat together as a group on the floor level, about fifty yards from the speaker's podium. Our positioning was done on purpose so that Marshall President Roland Nelson would be sure to see us as he delivered his keynote address. Wright (BUS president) and Shellcroft (a BUS cofounder) sat with other student leaders on stage.

A few minutes into Nelson's speech, Wright gave us a nod as he and Shellcroft approached the podium. Shellcroft interrupted Nelson's speech twice before he was allowed to speak. He explained the reasons for the protest as we stood up and remained silent with clenched fists raised high: the black power sign.

Before leaving, Shellcroft assured the near-capacity crowd at Gullickson Hall that black students were not hostile. This demonstration, he explained, was conducted to ensure that "our problem" would be made known to the entire university. When Shellcroft finished speaking, we tore up our programs and walked out in a peaceful manner. As the group departed, you couldn't help but feel the glares and stares coming from the audience. It was hard not to notice so many frowning white faces.

According to the student newspaper's account, Dr. Nelson didn't hesitate to address what the audience witnessed after the protesters left the building. "If you had experienced the things that they had, you might not be able to contain yourself either," the president said. The near-capacity audience applauded Nelson's statement.

Even though the demonstrators had vacated the premises, the protest was far from finished. The group maintained its single-file formation as we walked out of Gullickson Hall, which was located next to the football practice fields. We embarked on a twenty-five-minute march across campus to Old Main, the school's administration building. Some of us carried bricks, which may have been perceived by onlookers as a sign of belligerence. That was not the case. Those bricks symbolized the building space that BUS had been promised but had not received.

As we entered Old Main, our march became a foot-stomping exhibition. The echoing sounds reverberated throughout the building as people on the first floor came out of their offices to see what was going on.

Eventually we exited through the front door. The destination was the bust of John Marshall, located near the front entrance to the campus. MU is named after John Marshall who was the fourth Supreme Court chief justice of the United States (1801–1835).

As protesters gathered around the bust, those who carried bricks placed their bricks in a neat stack at the base of the bust. Larry Carter, a tight end on the football team and a Reserve Officers' Training Corps (ROTC) cadet, placed the last brick—painted black—at the top of the stack.

Later that semester, Marshall's administration made good on its previous promises and BUS finally got its long-awaited headquarters. The Student Relations Center, known affectionately as "the BUS station," was created to provide viable support programs for black students. Since its inception, the center has expanded its role to provide support services for women and international students.

By the start of the fall semester of '70, the university's Division of Student Affairs began to develop programming for the new center. Getting space in the Student Union was extremely gratifying. Through persistence and determination in dealing with the powers that be, BUS was now a full-fledged, fully recognized on-campus entity. It was a sweet victory for Marshall's black students..

"We had our place, our gatherings, and our plans," said activist Bill Dodson.

The rhythm and blues classic "We're a Winner" performed by the Impressions captured our feelings perfectly. It felt so good to see some tangible evidence that the BUS organization was finally starting to gain full acceptance on campus. This just made me want to shout, *"Thank you, Lord, 'cause we're moving on up!"*

A little over a year after the BUS protest, things got really tense between blacks and whites on campus (November 13, 1970 – the day before the plane crash). For whatever reason, everyone could feel something bad in the air, like that sinking feeling you get in your gut.

And the weirdest part? The tension boiled over because of an athletic contest.

When Black United Students took on the all-white Kappa Alpha fraternity in an intramural flag football playoff game, it became the unlikely crucible for the racial animus simmering beneath. The KAs, notorious for parading the Confederate flag—a blaring siren of prejudice to the black community— seemed to enjoy hoisting the flag with maddening pride. "That flag had no business being there. It's a racist symbol, and it produced undue tensions," said Bill Dodson, summing up the thoughts of many.

Flag football is supposed to be far less physical than football played with helmets and pads. Not on this day. Elbows weren't just thrown; they were weaponized. The clear aim? Inflict pain. The racial powder keg was about to explode, especially as officials appeared to be favoring the KAs. The crowd, half-black and half-white, was on edge—giving and receiving barbs. The hatred was palpable; you could almost taste it.

The constant display of Confederate flags in the stands was deeply offensive to black students. After the game, KA pledges ran through crowds of black students waving the flags, clearly an audacious taunt. They were practically begging for a reaction—and boy, did they get one. In the immediate aftermath, the scene resembled a battle zone more than a college campus. "It was like tossing a gallon of gasoline onto an already smoldering fire," described one spectator.

The brawl lasted for about 45 minutes and three white guys got knocked around so bad, they ended up in the hospital. But believe it or not, that was just the beginning. The cafeteria was where things went from zero to a hundred real quick. I heard from someone that everything spiraled out of control when a white woman lobbed a plate of ice cream in the air that landed in this black woman's afro. Of all things! This black woman, fury in her eyes, grabbed the other woman by the neck, and was about to ram her head through a glass panel at the salad bar. Even now, I still get shivers thinking about what might have happened if someone had not intervened. Meanwhile, down the corridor leading to the lobby area of Twin Towers dorm, the scene was reminiscent of two armies readying for war. Two white frats (Kappa Alpha and Pi Kappa Alpha) on one side, black students and black townspeople on the other. With the tension so thick, it felt almost suffocating. At any moment, it seemed that everything would explode into mayhem.

By this time, the city police had arrived on the scene just as Larry "The Governor" Brown, a football player known for his calming presence, stepped into the fray. Bill Redd recalled, "I remember the Governor jumping in the middle (of the crowd) and saying, 'Break this stuff up!' He pretty much let everybody know that the first blow thrown would have to come through him." What made Brown special was his unique ability to connect with anyone and everyone. It was like he carried this universal translator for human emotions. With that kind of gift, can you imagine if he had gotten into politics? Man, he'd probably be running the show! Can't imagine anyone not liking "the Governor."

Lucky for everybody involved that cooler heads prevailed during that face-off. But even after the immediate danger subsided, the fear lingered. The incident was a stark reminder of the racial hatred many black students had experienced growing up. For some, like Bill Dodson, the memories of racial confrontations were all too real. The sense of dread wasn't fleeting—it was pervasive, a sinister shadow looming over every black student's shoulder.

Rumors circulated that the KAs and Pi Kappa Alpha members from other schools would descend upon Marshall, seeking revenge. The black community was on high alert. "There was apprehension on our part," Bill Dodson admitted, reinforcing the severity of the threat. "After what happened on Friday, we didn't know how far things would go. So, we got the word out that nobody should go anywhere alone. We felt this was a real threat in which there would either be retaliation or confrontation. The 13th *did happen*. It was real. It just didn't get the airplay."

By sundown, the signs were undeniable: Marshall University was on the brink of a racial meltdown.

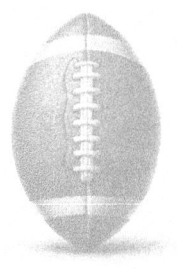

CHAPTER FOUR

The Moment that Shook Our World

November 14, 1970: The night was damp and chilly with a steady drizzle and dense fog. Looking out the window from my fifth-floor room at South Hall dorm, the lights from street traffic were barely visible from a block away. The usual nighttime glow from the houses in nearby neighborhoods was nonexistent. Weather conditions reminded me of scenes from those classic horror flicks shot in black and white. All that was missing was a silvery full moon and the eerie echoes of distant howls.

In piecing together the chain of events from that night, some things are still fuzzy. What I do remember is that somewhere between seven forty-five and eight o'clock I started hearing murmuring coming from the dorm hallway. I was relaxing and looking forward to attending an off-campus party later that evening.

There was talk of a plane crash at Tri-State Airport. Even though I realized it was about time for the football team to arrive on its return trip, it still didn't register that Marshall might be involved.

Gina (Starling) Gunn had no doubts. The day before the crash, Gina, a seventeen-year-old freshman, visited her dad who was the assistant athletics director at Marshall. Ed Starling made the team's travel arrangements and would've been on that flight, but he didn't go because of death in the family. "I saw all the (travel) information on my dad's desk," Gina explained. "So *I knew* it was the Marshall plane."

Once it was confirmed that it was the MU football team, there was no mention about survivors. Even so, there was still reason to hope that this would not be a worst-case scenario. Without realizing it, I was already in denial. I refused to consider that there would be no survivors. In the meantime, South Hall dorm was in a total frenzy and it seemed like everybody had this maddening sense of urgency to go to the airport. That's when I made a split-second decision. No, I would not venture to the crash site. I was frozen in fear about what I might encounter. Some images, once seen, scar you forever, and that was a pain I wasn't ready to bear.

Around half past eight, someone's shout echoed down the dorm hallway, "Phone call for Craig Greenlee!" Startled, I made my way towards the pay phone. As I picked up the receiver, I was surprised that it was my Aunt Ann. "Just watched the news," she whispered with a heavy heart. "I spoke to John and Winnie (my parents), and they told me there was no need for concern, that you had quit playing football. But you know how students can be at your age. Just wanted to hear your voice." Ann wasn't just any concerned relative; she was also a professor and black student program director at Cal-State Sacramento University. This dual role often made her witness to the unpredictable decisions college students frequently made without informing their families.

As our conversation progressed, what struck me the most was the depth of her sorrow. I could hear the raw pain in her voice for those promising lives cut short. "It just breaks my heart," she murmured. "So much potential, so many dreams... and now... They were all so young."

Elsewhere on another floor in my dorm, the pay phone continued to ring for several minutes. Folks were frantic in making contact with the school to find out about the players who were on that flight. Chuck Landon, a sophomore, rushed from his room and answered the phone. Larry "the Governor" Brown's sister was on the other end. She wanted to know if her brother was alive or not. Chuck was caught off guard and didn't know exactly how to answer. He knew there were no survivors. Nevertheless, he was extremely hesitant. Should he be the one to give her the bad news, even though it was the truth? He remained indecisive and decided to give what he felt was a safe reply: "Well, nobody's really sure right now. Nobody's been identified yet."

As he said good-bye, Chuck did his best to maintain a reassuring tone of voice. After hanging up, he immediately started second-guessing himself. "I hated myself a little bit," he said. "I should have had more courage to tell her that her brother had died. Things were so overwhelming that night."

Macie Lugo, a sophomore, was dating Larry "Dupree" Sanders, a standout cornerback and Marshall's best defensive player. Macie, the school's black homecoming queen known as Miss Black Pearl, was in her dorm room at Twin Towers when she first heard the news bulletin on the radio: *This is an emergency! There has been a plane crash at Tri-State Airport!*

Macie let out a shrill shriek heard by every resident on her floor. In spite of attempts to console her, she was convinced that her worst fears had come to pass. All that week, she couldn't shake the feeling that something would go wrong on that flight. "Right after I heard it, I told myself, 'Dupree is dead,'" Macie recalled. "It was the team's plane. I knew it in my soul. I remember asking myself if I could go on living without him."

At Pritchard Hall, the evening was shrouded in a somber haze. From her dorm room, Janice Cooley could hear the piercing wails and screams echoing from a nearby hallway, creating an eerie cacophony that chilled her to the bone. She felt an unsettling heaviness in the air, but was oblivious to its cause. As she tried to process the sounds, she received a summons, an unexpected message to rush downstairs and tend to a pressing phone call at the lobby desk. Heart racing and mind spinning with curiosity, she complied.

Holding the phone to her ear, Janice's body stiffened as she recognized the voice of a dear friend on the other end, the hesitance palpable. The words that followed, though delivered with caution, struck her like a hammer blow.

"Janice, heard anything about a plane crash?"

"What plane?" Janice's voice was quivering, a mix of confusion and fear.

"There's been a crash at the airport."

The brief pause that followed was torturous. "You don't think that's our plane do you?" Janice's words rushed out in desperation.

"Well ... it could be."

Denial clamped around Janice's heart, gripping it with a force that left her momentarily breathless. "No way! No way! No Way!," she exclaimed, each repetition acting as a desperate shield against the creeping reality.

Janice's mind raced with images of the last time she saw Art, their shared smiles, laughter, and whispers of promises. The very idea that such moments would now be consigned to mere memories was unfathomable. She refused, utterly and completely, to believe that the football team, that Art, her love, could be involved in such a horrific tragedy. With a heavy heart and tear-filled eyes, she departed from the front desk, making her way to the sanctity of her room.

Not long after, the soft knock on her door shattered the bubble of hope she'd formed around herself. The dorm mother, looking harrowed and trying her best to convey compassion, stepped in. Choosing her words with immense care, the dorm mother murmured, "I'm so sorry, Janice. The Marshall plane... everyone on board..."

But before she could finish, the devastating reality of the news shattered Janice's last threads of hope. The combination of pain, anger, and grief intertwined in a raging storm that threatened to consume her. Overwhelmed by emotion, without a moment's thought, Janice's hand connected with the dorm mother's face. The slap was loud, echoing the tumult within. Tears streamed down her face as she declared defiantly, "You don't know what you're talking about!"

In that heart-wrenching moment, all of Pritchard Hall bore witness to the indescribable pain of a soul shattered by loss.

Those who lived near the airport recall hearing an ear-splitting sound when Marshall's plane exploded. According to reports, the impact was so great that it caused houses in the surrounding area to shake. The crash scene did not stay isolated for long. Less than thirty minutes afterward, people swarmed the area. It took the authorities nearly two hours to finally clear the site of friends and family members of the victims, the news media, and onlookers.

Predictably, the plane crash produced an emotional tsunami of mourning and depression for everyone with any kind of connection to the school or the city.

Larry Isom heard about the crash and got a sick feeling in his stomach. Isom, a sophomore, was not an athlete, but he had more than a passing interest in Thundering Herd football. He and cornerback Bobby Joe Hill were best friends. In Isom's mind, it was unthinkable that Bobby, known to everyone as "Bee-Bop," might be dead. Soon after the news broke, Isom was among a group of twelve students who crammed inside two cars for the drive to the airport.

When they arrived, the main road was blocked off. The car Isom rode in pulled up beside one of the National Guardsman on duty. They would not be allowed to travel any farther. Before turning around and driving off, one of the students in the car insisted on gleaning more information from the guardsman. "Is this the football team's plane that went down?"

The guardsman responded with a company-line response. "I can't say. Right now, there's a lot that we just don't know."

Not satisfied, another student in the car spoke up. "Just tell us. Is it?"

The guardsman relented. "You all are going to get me in trouble. I'm not supposed to be telling you any of this. Yes, it is Marshall's football team."

The reaction to the news that nobody wanted to hear didn't settle very well. Wailing and screaming combined with moans of anguish pierced the night air. As the car turned around to leave, Isom heard shouting coming from the other carload of students. Somebody knew about an alternate route that would put them closer to the scene. It was the only accessible way to get to that part of the mountain where the crash occurred.

One car followed the other down this narrow dirt road, which wasn't too far from the highway. When the two carloads arrived, they quickly realized they were not alone. One side of the road was littered with cars, trucks, and ambulances. The flashing lights from the ambulances and the steady beams from the headlights of the other vehicles aided visibility to some extent.

Isom got out of the car and noticed a group of nearly a hundred people running in one direction. Instinctively, he followed the pack and bypassed a lot of folks on the way. Nobody seemed to care about the numbing cold or the muddy terrain, which caused more than a few folks to slip and slide as they moved about. The foggy conditions didn't help either. After running what seemed like a mile-long distance, Isom and the others turned off the road and ventured into the woods. Even though the area had been roped off by the emergency rescue team, it wasn't enough to keep people away. There were no state police, National Guardsmen, or volunteer firemen in the vicinity, so the crowd of onlookers continued to press their way through the dense woods.

It wasn't long before they came to a small hill. People started walking and running up this slightly steep incline. They were not prepared for what they saw when they reached the top: a front-and-center view of the Marshall plane lying at the bottom of the hollow. Debris and pieces of the aircraft were strewn over about a quarter of a mile. Some of the wreckage continued to burn for several hours after the crash.

"After a while, we realized we weren't going to find anybody," Isom said. "It was time to go. The people I rode to the airport with had already left. To get back to the school, me and a friend of mine had to ride in the trunk of a car."

Back on campus, mass anxiety reigned. There was still no "official" word about survivors. Time inched along at snail's pace. With every passing hour, it became more and more apparent that the unthinkable had occurred. Marshall had a major catastrophe on its hands.

Speculating about who might still be alive was not a topic I wanted to discuss. I needed to get away from the dorm. As I walked outside, folks seemed to be headed in one of two directions. The on-campus Christian Center was filled to capacity with students consoling one another. Gullickson Hall, the physical education building, served as a refuge. Gullickson, which served as temporary quarters for relatives of the crash victims, was overflowing with people who kept clinging to the hope that survivors would be found.

The entire world seemed to blur around me as I tried to wrap my mind around what had just happened. It was like my brain was stuck in a fog and I just couldn't think straight. The noise inside my head was so loud, everything else felt like a faint whisper.

How does one even begin to come to terms with a tragedy of such magnitude? The Marshall plane crash wasn't just a headline for me— it felt personal. The memories of shared practices, grueling training sessions, and countless locker room jokes played on a loop in my mind, all of them now tainted by the weight of this catastrophe. I felt a raw vulnerability, a sense of nakedness in the face of such unspeakable grief. My usual confident demeanor, the one I put on like a suit of armor every time I stepped onto the field, had crumbled. In its place was a shattered spirit, reeling from a tragedy that I couldn't even begin to understand.

The campus, once a sanctuary for me, now felt like a suffocating trap. Everywhere I looked, I saw familiar faces, lost and haunted. I knew they were seeking solace, a shoulder to lean on, a comforting word. But what comfort could I offer when I felt just as lost, just as devastated? So, I fled. Fled from the overwhelming wave of grief that threatened to swallow the entire campus. Fled from the burden of having to face others in their pain when I couldn't even come to terms with my own. My fiancee', Earnestine Ross, offered me sanctuary in her place, which helped me to get a better handle on my thoughts and emotions.

Yet, even there, escape was elusive. The shadow of the crash loomed large over every interaction. Each face I met, each voice I heard, echoed the same heavy sadness. The weight in the room was palpable, an oppressive force that seemed inescapable. As I sat on the couch, the television flickered with images and updates. These faces, ones I had laughed with, celebrated with, were now reduced to mere memories on a screen. The realization hit me like a sledgehammer.

This was a night stained with tears, with loss, with indescribable pain. The juxtaposition was jarring. How could life turn so dramatically, so cruelly, in just a matter of hours? Time seemed to stretch endlessly as the hours ticked by, each moment weighed down by the inescapable reality of the situation. I was trapped in a whirlwind of emotions—grief, anger, disbelief—and all I could do was let it consume me. In the midst of the storm inside my mind, one thought remained clear: life as I knew it would never be the same again. The plane crash left a deep mark. It always brings to mind how fate can twist in ways that we never anticipate.

Elsewhere in the city, a sizable crowd converged on one of the city's hospitals hoping and praying for the miraculous to occur. At the airport, a driver was placed on standby for the purpose of transporting injured people by shuttle bus to the hospital. In both cases, the waiting was in vain. By midnight, it was clear that there would be no need for those services.

Angela Dodson, the younger sister of Bill Dodson, first heard about the crash as she returned to campus after going home for the weekend. Angela, a fellow journalism major at Marshall, doesn't recall why she came back earlier than usual. It was around nine o'clock. The news—and the shock—were just beginning to set in. The area around the dorm where Angela lived and worked as a resident adviser had a massive overflow of people, a lot more than you would normally see on a Saturday night. Mattresses, pillows, and bed covers were piled in heaps everywhere: on the steps, in the lobby, in front of elevator entrances ... And people were bringing more of those items from upstairs to take over to Gullickson.

"I was aware of what had happened," Angela said, "but it took me a while to get a sense of what everyone was doing. It was a strange scene to see people throwing mattresses out (of their dorm rooms). As soon as I got on my floor, I heard screaming. It was a long night. I had thirty-two girls and everybody was crying. We had to take two ladies in for counseling that night."

According to news accounts, Gullickson Hall was frantic with activity. Doctors were on hand to treat frazzled students for shock. Athletic officials were on the phone lines trying to make contact with people who were supposedly not on that DC-9 jet. The coeds who weren't being treated, consoled, or counseled made themselves useful by passing out cups of coffee to students.

Cledis McQuay Hill dialed the phone number with a heavy heart and an anxious anticipation. She prayed for a sliver of hope, yearning for any news about her son, Bobby. Larry Isom, who was closer to Bobby than most in that dorm, found himself on the other end of that call. Before even picking up the phone, the weight of the truth pressed on his shoulders: Bobby was dead. Never in his life had Isom faced a reality this bleak. Losing someone, especially someone as young and full of life as Bobby, was foreign territory. He felt a tight knot in his stomach, his mind racing as he tried to find the right words.

Mrs. Hill's voice, tinged with hope, reached out from the other side, "Got any good news for me, Larry?" Time seemed to stand still for Isom. How do you shatter someone's world with just a few words? Taking a deep, steadying breath, he said, "No, Mrs. Hill, I do not." The stark reality of his words cut through the silence. The raw hurt in Mrs. Hill's sobs echoed the anguish Isom felt deep inside. Words couldn't fill the void created by such a tragedy. But Isom, wracked with sadness, wanted to be there for Mrs. Hill in any way he could. "If you need to come up here to West Virginia, I can make arrangements," he offered, hoping that his gesture might bring her some solace. But Mrs. Hill's response was hauntingly poignant. "There won't be any need for that," she whispered, voice breaking, "Bobby's gone, so what's the point?"

Two of the school's assistant football coaches—Mickey Jackson and Carl Kokor—heard the news Saturday night while driving back from Pennsylvania after watching Penn State play Ohio University. Both were assigned to scout OU, the next opponent on Marshall's schedule. Jackson and Kokor made repeated attempts to call Huntington, but all circuits were tied up. It took a few hours before they made contact with the Highway Patrol, which verified that the crash occurred and there was a possibility that there might not be any survivors.

Tired, sad, and stunned, the coaches got back in town around six o'clock Sunday morning. But instead of going home and getting some much-needed sleep, they immediately went to the football office. The first order of business was taking calls from family members of the crash victims to help bring some level of calmness to a chaotic situation. Quite a few folks on campus woke up much earlier than usual on this particular morning. Usually a lot of students get in right before the break of day on a Sunday morning after partying the previous night. In this case, the night before was unlike anything that any of us had ever dealt with.

Chuck Landon, his roommate, and his friends were up early and made a beeline to the nearest newspaper dispenser located one block from campus. He knew that if they got there before five o'clock when the delivery man made his drop-off, they were sure to get a copy of the Sunday morning paper that was sure to be sold out by nine o'clock. "When I got my copy and saw it in print, it made everything very real," he said.

I woke up around six o'clock that morning after falling asleep on the couch at my fiancée's apartment. As I walked back to the dorm, it was impossible to erase the memories from the previous night. This was a hard-to-swallow reality pill. The guys we had seen just two days earlier—the same guys we studied with, joked around with, partied with, and ate meals with— were gone, never to return. I picked up the Sunday newspaper and read the front-page headline: "Marshall Team, Coaches, Fans Die In Plane Crash." In my head, I knew it was true. But emotionally, it was difficult to accept. Quickly scanning all the headlines, I was shaken when I turned to an inside page that had a picture of every person who was on that flight. As I looked at the pictures, I could remember when most of these guys first came to Marshall.

Funeral Rites

FOR

Scottie Lee Reese

SATURDAY, NOVEMBER 21, 1970—2:00 P.M.

TOLIVER CHAPEL BAPTIST CHURCH
Reverend A. Charles Bowie, Pastor

My best friend ..... my best man

The first person I looked for was Scottie Reese, my best friend. He was to serve as my best man at my wedding in December. Scottie played outside linebacker and defensive end. We both came to Marshall in '68 and were starters on the freshman team. As sophomores, we were roommates on road trips. He didn't match up size-wise (six feet, two inches, 190 pounds) with others who played the same positions, but his field awareness and football IQ made him an exceptional player. Scottie would more than likely have had a career as an officer in the military. He was in Army ROTC at Marshall and was working toward earning an officer's commission by the end of his senior year of college.

As I continued to read and reflect, I found myself looking more at pictures of the players I was most familiar with—the members of the '68 freshman team.

- Bob Harris (quarterback): Excellent all-around athlete. Versatile enough to return kicks and make plays as a wide receiver or defensive back.
- Dennis Blevins (wide receiver): Pushed me to the limit when we ran the 400 meters and the 4 x 400 relay on Marshall's track team as freshmen. Every day in practice, I was determined to beat him, but could never do it.
- Willie Bluford (running back): Punishing inside runner was moved to linebacker for the '70 season. I admired Bluford's work habits. He didn't have breakaway speed, but had a knack for gaining the tough yards, and he rarely fumbled.
- Larry Sanders (cornerback). I'm glad that I never had to play against him in a game. During a scrimmage session, I got a taste of what opponents faced. I ran a route where I had to come back several yards to make the catch. Out of the corner of my eye, I saw that I had gotten some separation. I was open, or so I thought. When the ball arrived, so did Larry. His crunching hit left me feeling woozy for a few seconds.
- Roger Childers: Got married eight days before the crash. Starting strong safety on the '68 freshman team. Played linebacker the following year, then sat out the '70 season after undergoing

major surgery and served as team manager. Roger had planned to return to competition in '71.

The enormous sense of loss was not limited to the football team and most of the coaching staff. There were Marshall athletic administrators on that plane along with a number of boosters, which included prominent attorneys, doctors, business people, and civic leaders. Several folks, including two sisters who were Marshall cheerleaders, lost both parents that night.

In all, seventy-five lives were lost.

On the morning after the crash, something was amiss at First Baptist Church. A sanctuary usually buzzing with glowing warmth now felt dim, shadowed by a thick cloud of heartbreak. Gone were the harmonious songs and spirited prayers, replaced by an uncanny hush. Every pew told a story, filled to the brim not just with people, but with a town's collective grief. The air was thick, not just with sorrow, but with a palpable exhaustion—hundreds of eyes that had wept into the wee hours of the morning.

Marie (Williams) Redd, with wisdom beyond her sixteen years, stepped into this storm of emotion. While many of her classmates, along with some Marshall students and football players had once found refuge here, now there was an undeniable emptiness. Entering the sanctuary, the scene before her was unforgettable:

Pastor Charles Smith was pouring his heart out in fervent prayer. At the altar, a sea of college students clung to one another, their shared anguish palpable. The church was alive, not with joy, but with the raw emotion of grief. The sound of their heart-wrenching sobs painted a stark contrast to the typical joy-filled Sundays. "Everybody was in shock," Marie remembered. "People couldn't comprehend all that had happened from the night before. It was so sad, it was rough."

Yet, amidst the despair, the strains of a familiar hymn echoed in her mind. "Jesus Keep Me Near The Cross" is not a song of rejoicing, as Marie described. "It encourages us to get close to Jesus. It's very comforting to know that when someone leaves here (earthly life) and they're a believer, you know that they're going to a place where everything is perfect."

That day was a turning point for Marie. A brutal lesson in life's fragility, it also highlighted the true treasures: the connections we forge and the love we share. Despite the chaos, Marie realized that while life might be fleeting, it's the relationships and memories that give it depth and meaning.

The night after the crash, a memorial service was held at Memorial Field House, the off-campus arena where Marshall played its home basketball games. I knew well in advance that I would not be there. My feelings from Saturday night had not changed. The Field House was not where I wanted to be. That's not how a lot of other people felt. There were few vacant seats in the stands or on the floor level at the Field House (about 7,500 attended). Dignitaries representing the school, the city of Huntington, and the state of West Virginia were present. The heaviness of the occasion was readily evident.

The classic hymn "O God, Our Help in Ages Past" provided a sense of hope and assurance for a community in deep mourning. People listened to words of comfort, hugged one another, held hands, and did whatever they could to help in sharing the burden of grief and sorrow. "Everything seemed so quiet," said Gina (Starling) Gunn about the service. "There was such a feeling of numbness."

A day or so after the tragedy, several of Marshall's remaining football players expressed their desire to finish what their fallen teammates had started. After all, there was still one game left on the schedule. The only players left were those varsity guys who didn't make the trip because of injuries and members of the freshman team. They wanted to play Ohio University as a tribute to their deceased teammates.

The players left behind held a meeting to talk about the immediate future. About thirty-five players, mostly freshmen, were in attendance. Reggie Oliver, the freshman team's quarterback, recalls the wide range of emotions displayed in that meeting and the varying opinions as to what they should do as a team. Some wanted to play; some didn't. As an outward show of solidarity, the players signed a petition requesting that they be allowed to play that final game to close out the season.

They taped the petition on the wall next to Coach Tolley's office door. "We felt the need to make a statement," said Reggie. "We wanted to let it be known that this is what we wanted to do, if we were allowed. Once everybody's emotions got settled, we thought about things more rationally."

The desire to play the season finale was an understandable knee-jerk reaction to dreadful circumstances. The intentions were honorable, but it was a bad idea. For starters, freshmen were not allowed to play varsity football under NCAA rules. Plus, this decision never took into account that many of the players' funerals would be held the same day of that game and that people would want to attend those services. Not only that, but it's very unlikely that Ohio's Bobcats would have agreed to even play that game.

There was never a question about what the final decision would be. Game canceled.

"That was very courageous," said MU assistant coach Mickey Jackson in an interview, referring to the team's petition to continue the season. "They thought it would make a statement. But with so much going on, there was no way that anyone could focus on putting together a team to practice and prepare for a football game that week."

You couldn't go anywhere in the city and not be reminded of what happened. The sentence on the marquee at a local Holiday Inn summed things up succinctly: *"The Lord Giveth, the Lord Taketh Away."* Around town, flags were lowered to half-staff. Front-door entrances to city government offices and places of business were adorned with funeral wreaths. Unless you were there, you could never fully comprehend the gravity of grief that engulfed Huntington, West Virginia, in the days to follow.

It wasn't uncommon to see written messages on store windows that expressed condolences to the families of the crash victims. The university, city, and county governments shut down for two days. Scheduled events for the region were postponed or canceled. Marshall resumed its regular schedule by midweek, but it was hardly business as usual. I couldn't bring myself to talk about Scottie to my fiancée, Earnestine Ross. The three of us landed at Marshall back in '68. Earnestine was among the first wave of non-jock black students to attend predominantly white colleges in the South. It was a different time back then.

When the news of the plane crash reached us, it was surreal. For both of us, it's like we were caught in this... this state of "numbfoundedness." It wasn't tears, man. It wasn't loud cries. It was just this deep, silent turmoil inside, like an ongoing storm. We didn't even have the words, so we just held onto each other, silently. The weight of the pain, it was... indescribable

But there's one memory that lingers, as crisp as the morning air. Just three weeks before the tragedy, Scottie was one of the first to know about me and Earnestine deciding to tie the knot. We ran into him on a Saturday evening, right by the Student Union building. Funny, he was headed to this house party that we had just stepped out from. We broke our news, and without hesitation, Scottie said he'd be my best man. We were so excited about the wedding. It was all planned for December, right after final exams.

It was still next to impossible for me to get a grip, particularly when I thought about those teammates who came from the same hometown. Those "homies" grew up together and perished together. Thinking about that was heart-wrenching.

Cincinnati, Ohio, was home to four of the crash victims. Jim Schroer was the team trainer; the other three—Bob Harris, Jack Repasy, and Mark Andrews—had played at Moeller High School. There was a similar situation in Tuscaloosa, Alabama, where four players, all teammates at Druid High School, were laid to rest following a joint funeral held in the school auditorium. A huge crowd came to pay their final respects to Larry Sanders, Joe Hood, Freddy Wilson, and Robert VanHorn.

Bob Harris Sr., the father of quarterback/wide receiver Bob Harris, penned an inspirational letter of encouragement to the parents of players and others who were affected by the plane crash. The widely read letter was published in the local newspaper and Marshall's student newspaper, *The Parthenon*. This letter was written from the perspective of what Bob, Jack, and Mark would have said if they were able. Here's an excerpt from that message:

You have called us to Thy home in heaven and we come back home to Thee, our heavenly father. We pray to Thee, dear Father, for those we leave behind. Please bless them and give them the strength to uphold and keep safe the things we so dearly cherished while here on earth.

Help our parents, brothers and sisters and all those so dear to know that we are with them through Thee now and forever. Grant them the blessing to accept Thy will as we have. Hold them close to Thy bosom, dear God, so that they may know joy—not grief, as we answer Thy call.

Make them aware that our 20 years on earth were lived to the fullest, and were filled with love, warmth and happiness. We enjoyed an inner peace that comes from knowing we were loved by those whom we loved.

In the days immediately following the crash, there were still passengers who could not be positively identified. Bodies were burned beyond recognition when the Southern Airways DC-9 jet plunged into the side of a mountain at 160 miles-per-hour and exploded. Several days would pass before most of the bodies would be identified.

In many instances, parents and loved ones of the deceased players were forced to wait around before they could go into a dorm room and pack up personal belongings. Because of a Federal Aviation Administration mandate, they were prohibited from having access to players' rooms until each player who was an occupant of that room had been identified. In cases where deceased players were roommates, nobody could go in those rooms until both players had been properly identified.

The first few days following the crash, the South Hall lobby was flooded with the parents of players who were waiting to go to their sons' rooms. Some had to wait longer than others because of the time lapse in getting everyone identified. "It was like living in a funeral home," said Chuck Landon.

Scottie was one of the passengers who had not been identified immediately.

So, me and Sheila Callahan, who was also pretty tight with Scottie, decided to dive into his dorm room to find something that might help identify him. Rummaging through his clothes, memories hit me. Remember the whole homecoming drama? Oh, man, that was classic Scottie! Everyone and their momma was trying to pry out of him who he was taking to the dance. And Scottie? He was having a ball keeping it all hush-hush.

Finally, I mustered up the nerve to ask, "Alright, spill the beans. Who are you taking?" Scottie, with that mischievous glint in his eyes, replied, "Nunyah."

I was baffled. "Nunyah? What does that even mean?"

"It's 'nunnnnnn of ya' business," he smugly retorted.

That guy and his sarcasm! Always had a way of making things lively.

In the aftermath of the disaster, the school and community started going about the business of burying its dead. A television news director at one of the local stations commented how it became such a whirlwind to cover so many services in a short time span—thirteen in three days.

The process of identifying all seventy-five passengers was exhaustive. The medical staff had to rely on patches of clothing, dental records, fingerprints, key rings, watches, jewelry, and, in some cases, body parts to help identify victims. To help out with this task, it wasn't unusual for investigators to go by what friends and loved ones of the deceased remembered about the clothing the victims wore. In some cases, depending on other people's memories was the only means to help identify the charred remains.

All were identified with the exception of six players. Ten days after the crash, a joint funeral service was held at the Field House for Kevin Gilmore, Barry Nash, Allen Skeens, Tom Zborill, Dave Griffith, and Tom Brown. They were laid to rest at Spring Hill Cemetery in Huntington. The burial site serves as a lasting memorial to the '70 team.

In the DVD *Return of the Thundering Herd,* Coach Carl Kokor relives the most emotionally draining portion of that memorial service, which was held two days before Thanksgiving. During a scheduled moment of silence for the victims, one of Barry Nash's brothers left his seat and went to the front. In the stillness and quiet of the almost packed Field House, he ran from casket to casket and kept asking, *"Barry, is this you?"*

Seven days after the crash, I was in Waco, Texas, to bid Scottie farewell. I never considered taking the chartered bus that transported black students to several funerals in less than a week's time. (More on that in the next chapter.)

Yes, Scottie was gone, but he was still my best man. Even though he had Christmas vacation plans, he assured me that he would be there for my wedding. No disrespect to the other players, but for me, going to Waco was intensely personal. I felt a responsibility to go. As long as I had known Scottie, he had always proven to be trustworthy. Betraying someone's trust was something that Scottie Reese just didn't do.

Amidst the quiet mourning during the funeral, my eyes were fixed on the casket adorned with Scottie's jersey and the photograph beside it. About midway through the service, the weight of reality finally struck me: No. 83 was gone for good. The preacher's words? They escaped me. The hymns the choir sang? I couldn't recall. Even the journey to the cemetery, it's all a haze. A profound hush seemed to blanket my inner world.

Whenever I hear the song "Fire and Rain" by James Taylor, memories of Scottie flood in. I can still picture him standing at the Twin Towers dorm entrance, waiting to hop onto the team bus for the airport. Dressed in a sharp navy blue sport coat paired with pearly-white trousers, Scottie made his exit. But not before pausing, looking back at me. "See you when you get back," I casually called out. His silent nod in response was the last I saw of him. Little did I know, that would be our final exchange. Always thought I'd see Scottie again.

Scottie had a certain wit about him, and Bill Redd, a fellow student who didn't play sports, got more than a few doses of it. Bill and Scottie became thick as thieves after joining a college fellowship group at one of the local churches. There's this hilarious story about Scottie Reese that Bill loved to tell. One Sunday, they're bolting off campus, racing to church, and in the mad dash, Scottie forgets his socks. Bill, of course, couldn't let that go. "Hey Scottie," Bill teased, nudging his friend with a grin. "Going for a new church fashion trend? Shoes without socks?" Notorious for delivering witty comebacks, Scottie flashed a mischievous smile. "You think the Lord's up there checking out my footwear? Nah Bill Redd. He's busy seeing where my heart is."

Coming up with nicknames that "stick" was a Scottie Reese specialty. Whenever the team went to the dining hall, he noticed that offensive lineman Ed Carter ate more than everybody else. So, Scottie nicknamed him "Bodine," as in Jethro Bodine, the brawny character from the *Beverly Hillbillies,* a popular TV sitcom in the '60s. The Bodine character on TV was known for his ravenous appetite. The guys on the team, however, knew that Marshall University's version of Bodine would never take a back seat to Hollywood's Jethro. For example:

- After cashing a paycheck from his summer job at the local steel mill, Ed headed to the grocery store and bought a lot of chicken. That night he cooked and ate two whole chickens in one sitting.
- Most Sundays while school was in session, Ed and two other players routinely pooled their money to purchase a twenty-one-piece barrel of Kentucky Fried Chicken. The school cafeteria closed early on Sunday afternoon, so students were left to fend for themselves when it came to eating dinner on Sunday. In those days, the KFC barrel had bigger pieces of thighs and breasts to go with the wings and drumsticks. Ed and his comrades split the barrel three ways, which means they each had enough chicken for two meals.

"Whenever we went to the training table, I'd eat more food than probably anybody else on that team," Ed said. "That's why he started calling me Bodine. Even after the crash, the name stayed with me, but it was Scottie who started it."

Even though several decades have passed since the crash, people still remember Scottie. An anonymous writer posted the following blog entry about him on the *Herald-Dispatch's* website. As part of the newspaper's coverage in the weeks leading up to the premier of the movie *We Are Marshall*, readers were asked to share their memories from '70. The movie's storyline focuses on the crash's aftermath, the football program's restoration, and the process the community went through to heal itself.

> *"Several of my friends were players on the 1970 MU football team. When I got news of the crash, the first person that came to my mind was a very special person, Scottie. He always talked about his grandmother and how much he loved her. I'll always miss him."*

No facet of life at Marshall or the city of Huntington went untouched by the plane crash. You either had a close relationship with someone on that plane, or you knew someone who did. That's the norm in a close-knit college community. Marshall's football players were not housed in a separate dorm. They were assigned the same living quarters as regular students. It was the same way for meals. Because of that, there was a lot more interaction between athletes and regular students. A lot of meaningful personal relationships involving jocks and non-jocks developed.

That's why folks at Marshall were hurting in the worst way, especially on campus, a.k.a. "the compound." You either knew the football players personally or least knew *of* them. Everybody was overwhelmed by the bewilderment and anguish of the situation.

Recognized as the worst aviation disaster in the history of American sports, the Marshall crash has its share of haunting ironies.

A lot of the players were superstitious. They didn't like the idea of leaving town on Friday the 13th. It's been said that all during the week leading up to the road trip to East Carolina, several players expressed their concerns. Some called home to tell their parents that they might not return. Others left personal belongings with their girlfriends.

The weather conditions during the daylight hours of November 14 created a mood of gloom around Huntington. It rained on and off all day long. The sky was so dark that you got the impression that the sun had gone into hiding.

Meanwhile, the football team was forced to face its own depressing experience. The Thundering Herd suffered a heartbreaking 17–14 loss to East Carolina. Even worse, the game ended on a controversial call that went against Marshall. For the Herd faithful, it was a bitter defeat. Little did anyone know that the events that would occur *after* that game would compel everyone connected to the school and the city to forget all about football for the time being.

The night the Marshall plane went down will always be memorable. Not only was it the first and only plane trip the team had for that season, but it was the first time that Southern Airways had ever flown into Huntington. Prior to that night, Southern had never had one of its planes crash in twenty-one years of doing business. The flight crew for this journey was an experienced group. Pilot Frank Abbott had been with the airline since its inception. The average length of employment for the other crew members was about six years.

The National Transportation Safety Board conducted an investigation to determine the cause of the crash. An NTSB panel of inquiry convened for a hearing in Huntington, which lasted three days. It took five months for the panel to complete its findings. The NTSB issued its final report in April '72, but there is still no definitive explanation as to what caused the accident. Here's what the board concluded in its final report:

> The probable cause was the descent below Minimum Descent Altitude during a non-precision approach under adverse weather conditions, without visual contact with the runway environment. The Board has been unable to determine the reason for this descent, although the two most likely explanations are: a) improper use of cockpit instrument data; or b) an altimetry system error.

In layman's terms, it was either the instruments that malfunctioned; or it was a case in which the pilot and first officer misinterpreted the data provided by the instruments.

Mason Linker Jr., a seasoned commercial pilot, is well-acquainted with Tri-StateAirport. During a 30-year career with Piedmont Airlines, he landed at the Huntington airport around fifty times. While he's touched down in airports from Boston to Florida, Linker explains that West Virginia's mountainous landscape presents unique challenges for pilots. As he put it, "Some days it was a snap, on other days it wasn't. Even a 15-knot wind feels different in West Virginia compared to Florida, most likely because of the terrain."

On the night of the crash, adverse weather conditions made it problematic for landing, especially with Tri-State's shorter runway. Making matters even trickier, the airport lacked a glide slope, an instrumental tool for assisting pilots in making sure planes descend at the correct angle. "It's an aid that we really needed," Linker said. "Landing without a glide slope, particularly in bad weather, is seriously challenging."

For someone as seasoned as Linker, you'd think his insights on the Southern Airways Flight 932 crash would be invaluable. However, with admirable humility he observed, "It's been my experience that when I give an opinion, it turns out that I'm wrong a lot of the time. That's why I decline to speculate."

At the start of the '70 season, Marshall's team held so much promise. Fairfield Stadium, the Thundering Herd's home field, got a much-needed facelift with added seating and refurbished locker rooms. The playing field was converted from natural grass to AstroTurf. Marshall celebrated with a stomp-down victory in its season opener against Morehead State. This team had its share of studs, but the talent level wasn't quite the same once you got past the starting lineups.

As the season progressed, injuries and the lack of depth took a severe toll, and it really showed in the win-loss record. Entering the East Carolina contest, the Herd, 3–5 at the time, still had a shot at having a break-even season if it won its final two games. For a school that had finished on the downside of .500 for four consecutive seasons, ending the '70 campaign at 5–5 would have signaled humongous progress. Marshall posted a 3–6 record in its tragic season. In four of those losses, the average margin of defeat was 3 ½ points.

Still, there's another ironic twist to this story: In early October, the Thundering Herd, along with other college teams around the country, paid homage to the Wichita State football team. Marshall observed a moment of silence during its pregame meal prior to playing Xavier University of Ohio. Wichita State flew two planes for a road game at Utah State and one of the planes crashed, killing twenty-nine people, which included thirteen players. Six weeks later, Marshall met the same fate. But compared to Wichita State, MU's losses were far more devastating.

In a way that was totally unexpected, the crash had a calming effect on race relations at Marshall. In '70, blacks comprised about 3 percent of a student-body population of about 7,500. The football team's forty-seven-man roster for that season was 30 percent black.

Three Students Hurt In Fight

Three Marshall University students were injured Friday in a fight which started shortly after the finish of a football game between two fraternities on the university's intramural field, city police reported.

Police made no arrests in the 5:40 p.m. incident.

Taken to the Chesapeake & Ohio Railway Hospital were Donald H. Saller, 20, of 1434 5th Ave.; John Onderko, 20, of 1533 4th Ave.; and Charles Ward, 19, of 723 W. 18th St.

Mr. Saller was admitted in satisfactory condition with a severe cut of the right chest while the other two were treated for smaller multiple cuts and released. Police said knives' apparently were used.

One of the victims reported being struck over the head with a bottle and the others said they were jumped from behind by about five subjects as they were walking away from the field.

The above article is about the Friday the 13th melee that could have easily escalated into a bloody race riot on the Marshall campus.

Given what happened on Friday the 13th, many of us believed we were on the brink of a full-blown race riot at Marshall University. But before the night of the fourteenth ended, moods, emotions, and outlooks changed dramatically. Everybody suffered indescribable losses that transcended race and heritage. Nobody was thinking about any racial beef. It was as if the Friday fights had never happened. Folks were too busy grieving and making plans to attend funerals. The recollections are still vivid in many people's minds, including a Huntington resident who submitted a blog entry for the *Herald-Dispatch* newspaper's website. The writer, who chose to remain anonymous, described how the crash played a pivotal role in black-white relations on campus.

> I remember the night oh too well. A number of us had been working to make sure a scheduled demonstration regarding racial intolerance on the campus would be peaceful. (Black student activists) Bill Redd, Bill Dodson and Angela Dodson were in dialogue with a number of white student leaders to avert any violence. The news came on and all talk of demonstrations, of race, of racial inequality stopped. We were a family, and we had lost so many of our family members. As a local resident, I not only lost campus friends and classmates, but members of the community. Not a day goes by that I don't think about them and my heart grieves.

The legacy of the team that perished goes way beyond wins and losses. It's my belief that this group had a divine calling to fulfill a greater destiny. The racial turmoil brewing on campus from those Friday fights was totally squashed because of what happened on the night of November 14. Racial and cultural differences really didn't matter anymore. The sorrow and shock were so complete that everybody forgot all about Confederate flags and racial hatred.

This wasn't a black thing.

This wasn't a white thing.

This was a death thing, and death does not discriminate.

Grieving people were too busy trying to make sense of it all. So, in ways that nobody could ever imagine, Marshall's '70 football team became an agent for peace between the races.

*****

The '70 team is generally recognized as the group that would have ultimately put Marshall on the college football map. What folks might not be aware of is that this team was composed mostly of players recruited by Perry Moss in '68 and '69. There was some serious talent onboard, which included genuine NFL prospects. Here are some brief notes on the deceased players who I believe would have played professionally.

- Larry Sanders–Savvy defensive back, strong on solo pass coverage, noted for delivering skull-busting hits. Big and muscular at six feet, three inches, 195 pounds. Excelled at providing run support. Played cornerback in college, could have easily transitioned to safety at the next level.
- Joe Hood–Running back, had a rare combination of size, sprinter's speed, and graceful moves. Reminiscent of Gale Sayers in his prime. Exceptional receiver. Joe had little or no body fat at six feet, two inches and 200 pounds. Clocked at 4.3 seconds in the forty-yard dash. Absolute nightmare for any defender trying to take him down in the open field.
- Dennis Blevins–Big wide receiver (six feet, two inches, 190 pounds), legitimate deep threat with excellent hands. Tough to cover because of his leaping ability, physicality, and 4.5 seconds speed in the forty-yard dash. Tireless worker, possessed exceptional stamina.
- Jack Repasy–Consummate possession receiver, speed was not his calling card. Compensated by running precise pass routes. Rarely dropped anything thrown his way.
- Art Harris–Smooth-talking running back known as "Broadway," played much bigger than his size (five feet, nine inches, 195 pounds). Highly recruited by most of the major colleges in the

East and Midwest. Rugged enough to run between the tackles, quick enough to make tacklers miss, swift enough to run past most defenders. Reliable receiver. Playing style similar to Austin Ekeler of the Los Angeles Chargers.

- Marcelo Lajterman–Strong-legged sophomore routinely kicked field goals from fifty yards out in practice. Booted a forty-seven-yard field goal vs. Western Michigan in his only season of varsity competition. Soccer-style kickers were still relatively new to American football in the early '70s. If he had completed his college career, Marcelo, born in Argentina, had the skills to rank among the best kickers of his day.

- Ted Shoebridge–Big-play quarterback, blessed with superb field vision and an uncanny sense of timing. Had scholarship offers from many of the nation's top programs. Double threat as runner and passer. If he didn't make an NFL team, would have found a home in the Canadian Football League because of his mobility.

Marshall University has made its mark in the NFL. But think about it: that influence could've been felt a lot sooner. The tragic plane crash robbed many talented players of their future, and I genuinely believe that had they lived, they would've paved the way to the NFL for Marshall. It's not just about the likes of Carl Lee, Troy Brown, Chad Pennington, Randy Moss, Byron Leftwich, and Ahmad Bradshaw. The Herd had the potential for greatness long before these names became synonymous with NFL success. The legacy is deep, and the talent was always there.

Lee was a three-time All-Pro cornerback with the Minnesota Vikings, and Brown earned three Super Bowl rings as a wide receiver with the New England Patriots. Pennington started at quarterback for the New York Jets and Miami Dolphins.

Moss, a record-breaking receiver and easily the most recognizable of all the former Marshall players, was inducted into the Pro Football Hall of Fame in 2018. Leftwich quarterbacked the Jacksonville Jaguars for five seasons prior to moving on to Atlanta, Tampa Bay, and Pittsburgh (back-up QB when Steelers won Super Bowl XLIII). In his fourth NFL season in 2010, Bradshaw blossomed as one of the league's most productive backs with 1,235 rushing yards and eight touchdowns. He turned pro after his junior season of college in 2007. As a rookie, he was a key contributor in the New York Giants stunning upset of New England in Super Bowl XLII.

The success of individual players at the professional level can have a profound impact on the success of a college program. Recruiting more upper-echelon athletes gives schools a better shot at winning consistently. That's especially critical for schools who are card-carrying members of college football's bluebloods.

Year in and year out, the big boys – the Alabamas, the Georgias, the Ohio States compete in the national playoffs or play in bowl games. The payoff? They fare better in the recruiting wars to sign the top players in the country. Loading the roster with gifted players is the difference-maker between teams that are good every once in a while as opposed to teams that are always ranked among the nation's Top 25. Powerhouse programs do not rebuild; they simply reload.

Football-wise, Marshall is not at the same competitive level as schools in the SEC, Big 10 ACC, or PAC-12. But that doesn't mean Herd football hasn't served as a springboard for several NFL careers. When Marshall won national championships (NCAA Division I-AA) and bowl games after moving up to Division I-A (now known as the College Bowl Subdivision), the Herd was able to systematically stockpile talent, which enabled the program to consistently contend for championships. Marshall's on-the-field success attracted a greater number of players with pro potential. The end result: Herd football had its heyday in the '90s.

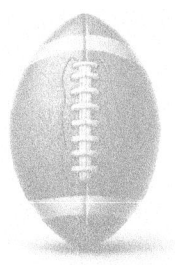

CHAPTER FIVE

Pilgrimage of Heartache

Following the heart-wrenching plane crash, a remarkable tale of oneness emerged. Black United Students rallied to collect funds through private donations, ensuring they could pay tribute to the black players who tragically perished. Some took to the skies and headed for Texas, some drove by car to New Jersey, and others embarked on an intense 1,500-mile journey over just four-and-a-half days. Their path? A heart-rending circuit through Bluefield (West Virginia), Atlanta (Georgia), Tuscaloosa (Alabama) and Greenwood (South Carolina). Along the way, the group attended a wake and three funerals. All aboard for the Homegoing Caravan!

CRAIG T. GREENLEE

MARSHALL UNIVERSITY
HUNTINGTON, WEST VIRGINIA 25701

STUDENT PERSONNEL
PROGRAMS

STUDENT RELATIONS CENTER

BUS AND AIRLINES SCHEDULE

SCOTTIE REESE

Saturday, 1:00 at the
Tolliver Chapel Bapt. Church
Waco, Texas

Craig Greenlee
Sheila Callahan

LV Fri. - Charleston 11/20/70
United #641 - LV 8:15 AR
Atlanta AR 9:20 LV EA #257
11:15 AR Dallas 12:07 LV
Trans Texas 1:40 AR Waco 2:11
Staying at Holiday Inn

BOBBY HILL

St. Matthews Bapt. Church
Saturday, 11:00 AM.
Dallas,Texas

Larry Isom
Brenda Gravely

Larry Isom
LV Fri. - Charleston 11/20/70
United #641 - LV 8:15 AR
Atlanta 9:20 LV EA #257 - 11:15
AR 12:07 (Return unscheduled)

Brenda Gravely
(Same as above)
LV Sun Trans. Tex #685 8:35 AM
AR Waco 9:06 LV Mon T Tex #682
6:30 AM AR Dallas 7:00 LV
#790 at 7:45 AR Atlanta 10:27
LV United #796 12:25 AR Chas.
2:19 (Need Pick up - same return
for Greenlee, Callahan, Gravely,
Smith. Staying at the Central
Holiday Inn.

LARRY BROWN

Saturday at 11:00 AM
Lindsey Street Bapt.
North Ave. and Linsey St.
Atlanta, Georgia,
Rev. Alexander,
Sister 404-525-8792
Mrs. Zela White 524-1267
Iris Duckwyler
John Ndega

LV Fri. Charleston 11/20/70
United #641 - 8:15 AR Atlanta
9:20 AM.
LV Atlanta Sunday 11/22/70
United #675 - 7:55 AR Chas.
8:57 PM. (Pick up)

Here are two pages from the itinerary of the "Homegoing Caravan," a bus trip in which Marshall's black students attended a wake and three funerals for seven of the 10 black players who died in the plane crash.

MARSHALL UNIVERSITY
HUNTINGTON, WEST VIRGINIA 25701

STUDENT PERSONNEL
PROGRAMS

STUDENT RELATIONS CENTER

LARRY BROWN

Joyce Thomas
Neal Borgmeyer

Via Greyhound 11/19/70 7:15 PM.
AR 11/20/70 1:00 PM. LV 11/22/70
(Unscheduled) Staying at the
Paschal Motel, Tel. 577-3150 830
Hunter Street, Atlanta

Bus will arrive 11/20/70 at
11:15 at Andrew Funeral Home
LV 12 Midnight for Tus.,Ala.

WILLIE BLUFORD

Eloise Hocker
Carolyn Brown
Teresa Harmon

Sunday at 2:30
Rev. James A. Gray
682-3382

LV 11/21/70 Via Car 5AM
LV 11/22/70 4:00 PM.
Go to Maxwell Funeral Home -
will take you to Motel

Bus will arrive 12 Noon. Go
directly to the Robinson & Son
Funeral Home on Maxwell Ave.
Tel. 223-5125

ART HARRIS

Walter Garnett
Janice Cooley
Maurice Cooley
Claude Smith

LV 11/18/70 at 8:00 AM for
Passiac, New Jersey. Return
11/22/70 via car - Walter
Garnett

LARRY SANDERS
JOE HOOD
FREDDIE WILSON
ROBERT VAN HORN
DENNIS BLEVINS
LARRY BROWN
WILLIE BLUFORD

Via Greyhound Bus LV South Hall
11/20/70 5:00 AM - Ar Bluefield
10:00 AM LV 1:00 PM. Dinner in
Chattanooga, Tenn. AR Atlanta,
11:00 PM. LV Midnight AR Tus.
4:30 AM Sat. LV Sun 5:30 AM
AR Greenwood 12 Noon LV 6:00 Pm
AR Huntington 3:30 Mon AM.

ACCOMMODATIONS

1. Tuscaloosa Otis Flucker

Telephone
Contact   Stillman College
Orouke 759-4555

"Homegoing" is a time for jubilation. Yes, there is sorrow and sadness for those who have passed away. Yet there's cause for much joy because they have *gone home* to be with the Lord for eternity.

Gina (Starling) Gunn wanted to attend some of the funerals, but her parents ordered her to stay at Marshall. The Starlings had just returned to West Virginia after burying Gina's grandfather in Mississippi a week earlier. Gina had just turned seventeen so her parents were concerned about her ability to cope with so much tragedy in such a short period of time. "When I told them I was planning to go, they said, 'No way,'" Gina said. "I understood where they were coming from. They felt it was in my best interest to stay. Still, I was extremely upset with them."

It's still amazing to realize that this trip was put together so quickly. Local ministers Reverend Charles Smith of First Baptist Church and the Reverend Dick Miller of Ebenezer United Methodist Church were instrumental in planning the trip and helping to facilitate the fund-raising effort.

To appreciate how quickly this all came together, consider the timeline of events. The crash occurred on a Saturday night; by Wednesday, all but the most minor details had been worked out for the lengthy trek to actually take place. The chartered bus left Marshall's campus on Thursday night for Dennis Blevins's funeral the next day in Bluefield. The group returned to Huntington early Monday morning of the following week after attending services for Willie Bluford in South Carolina—the fourth and final stop.

"At first it seemed like a wild idea," said Joe Bundy, a freshman who went on the trip. "No rational person would ever think it could be done. We had something like forty-eight hours to raise all this money to secure a bus for the trip south, airplane tickets for people to fly to Texas (Dallas and Waco), and travel money for students to go to New Jersey. College students are idealists. We wanted to do whatever we could to make it happen."

The day after the crash, the school started assigning students to assist the parents and relatives of the players who died in the plane crash. When the relatives came to town, they were housed at a hotel near campus. Most had trouble getting any sleep. So, they stayed up and talked, and talked—all night long. During one of those conversations, the suggestion was made to find a way for students to attend as many funerals as possible.

Bundy, who was assigned to assist Wilbert Wilson, father of tight end Freddy Wilson, found some relief from his grief in fulfilling his role. "Rather than think about how bad I felt about losing a homeboy (Dennis Blevins), my focus changed," he said. "I began to think a lot more about Mr. Wilson and what he was going through. This situation allowed me to be strong for that parent. Our role was to keep the parents lifted up. You didn't want to break down in front of them."

Getting fifty-plus seats filled on the chartered bus was not a problem. There was a strong sense of obligation to go on this trip. Folks had a burning desire to pay their final respects. Nobody ever said it, but all of us knew it was the appropriate thing to do. Whites were not barred from the caravan. It just turned out that no white folks signed up to go. The school made sure that Marshall would be represented at every player's funeral by assigning various faculty and staff members to attend designated services.

Several campus organizations held memorial services for all the crash victims. But among the blacks at Marshall, there was a unique affinity because of skin color and culture. Call it a sign of the times. It was a time in which blacks were the small minority on white college campuses, but very vocal in helping to pave the way for blacks' inclusion into every facet of student life. Marshall was no different. Back then, the black pride movement was at its peak. The soul hit "Say It Loud: I'm Black and I'm Proud" by James Brown became an anthem for blackness during that era.

"Marshall was a very small community," said Angela Dodson. "There were only a few of us (black students). To lose ten at one time was a big dent. In the midst of all the confusion and shock, we needed to do something active or proactive to try to process all that had happened and be part of it."

The most unique aspect of this trip was the kaleidoscope of emotions experienced by the passengers as they traveled from one funeral site to another. There were upbeat moments accompanied by laughter and horseplay—and always lots of spontaneous singing. By the end of the journey, it's safe to say that there were few onboard who didn't know at least one stanza of the black gospel song "We've Come This Far by Faith." All during the trip, caravan passengers sang spirit-lifting songs that reinforced a message of hope that some way, somehow, everything was going to be alright.

Audience participation on the bus trip didn't end with a song. As a means of coping, the passengers—one by one—got out of their seats and shared their fondest memories of the players who died. These testimonial-style presentations helped everyone on the bus to learn more about the human side of these deceased athletes.

Melancholy moments were to be expected. Every time the bus would get within forty to forty-five minutes of arriving at the next funeral stop, the mood would change dramatically. Bus riders went from being jovial to being in mourning. At those times, silence gripped the atmosphere. With the exception of some quiet chatter here and there, the only sound was the barely audible hum of the engine as the bus motored down the highway. This aura of quietness remained when passengers boarded the bus after attending a homegoing. The silence would last for as long as an hour or two. At times, the stillness was so obvious that you could hear a mosquito breathe.

These extremes in shifting emotions played out time after time over the course of the journey. "At one point, you felt terribly sad," said Joe Bundy. "But then you felt a closeness, a togetherness, a love for each other; and you felt how *everybody* was holding up everybody else."

In the midst of the prevailing silence and heaving sighs, Larry Carter's voice emerged as a beacon of relief. A three-year starter at tight end, Larry exhausted his college eligibility a year earlier. The year of the crash, he was completing coursework to graduate and start his military career as an Army officer. Everytime the group embarked on another funeral stop, the mood on the bus was somber, reflective, and heavy with sadness. Just when the air inside felt almost suffocating with sorrow, Larry took up the bus microphone. It was like he had an innate sense to know when everybody needed a break. In that familiar tenor voice of his, so smooth and jazzy, he'd ask, "*What's happenin' and thangs?*"

A small chuckle, a hushed giggle, the sound was infectious. Larry had a knack. It wasn't that he was taking away the pain; he was just providing moments of comfort. Every now and then, someone would try to catch a nap between stops. Snoozing, however, made every rider an easy target. Larry's playful jabs at people's sleepy faces, had the whole bus bursting into laughter.

For Larry Carter, being part of the Thundering Herd wasn't just about playing football. It was about understanding and brotherhood. The Homegoing Caravan needed him, his light moments, his jests. It wasn't about making everybody forget, but about helping everybody remember that in the darkest of times, there's a need for a ray of light, a chuckle, a shared moment of humanity. Having Larry Carter around made the trip just a bit more bearable.

The caravan followed a hectic schedule during its first full day. The group made two of its four homegoing stops, beginning with the services in Bluefield and ending with a wake in Atlanta on Friday night.

Those in attendance at Blevins's funeral represented a balanced racial cross-section of mourners who filled the pews to near capacity. Blevins, a revered three-sport star, was one of a handful of black Catholics in Bluefield at that time. While his church family was overwhelmingly white, Blev's kinship ties and other social connections were rooted in the black community.

"The first funeral was the hardest because it was the first," said Paulette (Dodson) Scott, a junior in '70. "With the setting and surroundings, you were reminded that this is real, that this young man is gone. I can't say that things got any better as we went to the other funerals. By the time we had gone to three services, you just learned to deal with it and you adjusted as best you could."

*****

The caravan journeyed on, charting its course towards Atlanta. It's not an easy feat, traveling such distances as part of a large group. As hours passed, discomfort was evident in the faces of its weary passengers. Seats, initially inviting, felt rigid and unyielding. Conversations dwindled, replaced by a collective introspective silence.

The cloak of night provided a mixture of solace and disorientation. But as the skyline of Atlanta began to take shape, illuminated by twinkling city lights, it was clear they had arrived late. The clock hands rested at around 11:30 p.m., well beyond what one would consider regular business hours. Yet, against this backdrop of night and weariness, the funeral home stood as a beacon of compassion. They had made special arrangements, ensuring their doors remained open for this caravan to pay their respects to Larry "The Governor" Brown. The time constraints were evident; with a mere forty minutes spent at the funeral home for Larry's wake. The schedule was tight because the group had to be in Alabama the very next day for another funeral service.

Even though the visit was brief, the impact was profound. The significance of the presence of Marshall's black students was palpable. As Bundy observed, "We didn't spend much time there, but you still got the sense that us being there was very important to Larry's family. We came away feeling like we were able to help in a tangible way." This sentiment echoed among the caravan members too. Even in fleeting moments, their presence, their shared sorrow with Larry's family, created an ineffable bond, a testament to the strength of shared humanity in the face of grief.

*****

Tuscaloosa, Alabama: Reggie Oliver took a deep breath, his heart overflowing with emotion. The Druid High School auditorium was filled with an unmistakable heaviness, as the weight of grief settled over the gathered crowd. With over 2,500 attendees, the room was at capacity, with many standing shoulder to shoulder, their faces etched with pain and remembrance. The portraits of Larry Sanders, Joe Hood, Robert VanHorn, and Freddy Wilson were stark, silent reminders of a bond cut short. Memories of their laughter and their dreams, including their shared pact to turn Marshall University into a football powerhouse, came flooding back.

This agreed-upon mission was what had driven them through countless hours of practice and shared sacrifices. It was what had brought them closer, binding them together in a brotherhood that transcended the sport. Now, it was a dream unfulfilled, a mission left incomplete.

As Reggie made his way down the aisle, he was pulled into a vortex of sorrowful embraces and questions, each one slicing a little deeper into his soul. The pressing crowd, the anguish in their eyes, and their insistent need for answers turned his vision into a narrow tunnel of pain. Reggie's tunnel ended abruptly when he felt a repeated tug on his sleeve. He looked down into the eyes of a grieving mother, eyes that were pools of raw emotion. When she spoke, her voice was barely a whisper, a fragile wisp of air borne out of unimaginable pain. "All I want to know is—is that my son in there?"

Reggie's heart tightened. This pain, this unbearable weight of loss, was mirrored in her eyes. The starkness of her question felt like a punch to the gut. The depth of her anguish was evident for everyone to see, even if her words were only for him. He took a moment before responding, trying to find words that would give her some measure of comfort. But no words seemed sufficient. The heavy burden of that conversation would forever remain between them, a painful secret shared in the midst of collective grief. The service passed in a blur for Reggie, the mother's haunting question echoing in his mind. By the time it ended, he felt numb, lost in the midst of his grief.

A few hours after the service, Reggie was still trying to process the day's events when the phone rang, snapping him back to the present. Picking it up, he recognized the voice immediately—it was the father of his recently buried friend, the same man married to the heartbroken mother he had spoken to earlier.

"Hey Reggie," he started, his voice strained and thick with sadness. "Look, I know how tight you two were," he paused, letting out a deep breath. "But my wife is really having a hard time right now. She's used to seeing the both of you together all the time. When she sees you, she automatically thinks of him. So, it would be best if you don't come over to the house."

Reggie's heart ached anew. His mere presence was now a source of immense pain for the grieving mother. He swallowed hard, struggling to keep his voice steady. "I understand," he replied, the burden of his grief evident in his voice. The loss of four treasured friends, the overwhelming sorrow of that day, would forever be etched in Reggie's memory. It was a stark reminder of the fragile threads that bind us to one another and the profound impact of those bonds when they are severed.

Ed Carter didn't ride the chartered bus but traveled to Alabama by car with some Marshall basketball players. He remembers an incredibly gut-wrenching moment. During the service, a grieving parent of one of the deceased players cried out in anguish. "Why did my son have to die in that crash? Why were the others not on that plane?

That's not something you'd expect to hear at a funeral. All-consuming grief can cause people to make comments they wouldn't ordinarily make. Ed recognized that the reference to "the others" included him and those players who did not travel to East Carolina. "I could tell it was directed at me, even though nobody said anything to me specifically," Ed Carter said. "It was emotional and very understandable. I had no reaction. I did not say anything back."

At Cedar Oak Memorial Park, the landscape was blanketed with mourners. An estimated crowd of 800 had gathered to say their final farewells. While the preachers shared their heartfelt words, a lone figure began to distance herself from the crowd. It was Macie Lugo, the girlfriend of Larry Sanders, one of the departed players. Her face was an enigmatic facade, betraying no emotion. Trailing closely behind her was Murrial (Jarrett) Ruth, Macie's best friend.

As the duo found themselves about fifty yards away from the throng of mourners, Murrial locked eyes with Macie, their gazes intense and unwavering. The deep lines of worry on Murrial's face contrasted sharply with Macie's unreadable expression. "Talk to me, Macie," she implored. "What are you feeling? Why aren't you crying? Why aren't you showing any emotion? *Please* don't keep this bottled up inside you!"

Macie offered no response, her silence echoing louder than any words. Feeling the weight of the moment, Murrial took Macie's hand, leading her further away from the sea of people. They eventually reached their car, and the journey was marked by an unbroken silence, punctuated only by the soft shuffle of their feet. Reflecting on that poignant day, Murrial remarked, "At the cemetery, I tried to get Macie to let her emotions out. But by then, she was already in that quiet, stoic mode. It was easy to see that this (death of Larry Sanders) was the hurt of her life. I don't think she ever got over it."

Al Evans and several of his Marshall schoolmates endured some hardships on the trip to Tuscaloosa, but difficulties did not deter them from reaching their destination. Evans developed a deep and lasting bond with Freddy Wilson, who frequently went home with him on weekends during the summer months.

Evans and a second carload of Marshall students took off for Alabama to attend the services, and he rode in Freddy's car. The twelve-hour trip took much longer than it was supposed to. Freddy's '62 Ford Falcon broke down on the way, and it didn't help that no one among the traveling crew could read a road map correctly. They kept getting lost, which added a few more hours to their already lengthy journey through the South.

Since only one of the cars was now operable, the passengers and luggage from Freddy's Ford were stuffed into a second vehicle, so now there were seven passengers riding around in cramped quarters like sardines packed in a can. Once they arrived in Tuscaloosa, they stopped at an apartment complex to verify where they would stay while in town. They were not part of the caravan, so they were responsible for making their own overnight sleeping arrangements.

While they were inside one of the apartments in the complex, thieves apparently labeled the car as an easy mark because of the out-of-state license plate. They broke into the car and stole every piece of luggage. The local Jaycees made good of a bad situation and provided some funds to purchase apparel so that Evans and the others had clothes to wear to the funeral.

"It wasn't a very comfortable ride," Evans recalled. "At that point, nobody really complained. We just did what we had to do. Your mind wasn't on anything you might have to deal with. Freddy was a big, friendly, good-natured guy. You knew he would always have your back."

The tragic deaths of the four athletes led the community to question why they chose to travel so far from home to go to college. There was the pervasive sentiment among the folks in "T-town" that Sanders, Hood, VanHorn, and Wilson should never have had to leave the state to play prime-time college football in the first place.

Skin color was the reason why. In the late '60s, white colleges in the South would not recruit blacks. In Alabama, it was accepted as fact among the coaches that white college football fans were not ready to embrace black athletes. For blacks who wanted to play at a predominantly white school, the only options were to go north or to the West Coast.

It is generally believed that the racial complexion of college football changed drastically in '70 when the integrated University of Southern California crushed an all-white University of Alabama team in a nationally televised game. Sam "Bam" Cunningham, a black fullback, bulldozed the Crimson Tide with 135 rushing yards and two touchdowns in a decisive 42–21 victory. In the years to follow, Southern white schools began to tap into the talent pool that had been the exclusive domain of the historically black colleges. 'Bama signed its first black player—Wilbur Jackson—months before the start of the '70 season. Wilbur, however, was reduced to being a spectator in his first year of college. NCAA rules prohibited freshmen from playing varsity football and basketball in those days.

The city of Tuscaloosa welcomed the caravan contingent with open arms and Stillman College eagerly accepted its role as host. Stillman, a predominantly black school, served a full-course breakfast buffet and made its dorm rooms available for sleeping quarters. The hospitality didn't stop there. After the joint funeral, some Stillman students hosted a get-together for the Marshall group that night.

In some cultures, going to a party just hours after attending a funeral is viewed as being grossly inappropriate. In other cultures, however, it's the exact opposite. "To me, it was like the goal Stillman students had was to help ease the pain we were going through," said Lawson Brooks, a Marshall freshman at the time of the tragedy. "As we sat around and talked, we felt like the guys would want us to go on. They wouldn't want us to dwell on the sadness of it all. It was a strange kind of feeling. I saw the party more as an outgrowth of their love for us. The students at Stillman really reached out to us."

*****

Of all the caravan stops, Greenwood, South Carolina, was clearly the most rural. No city skyline. No expressway. No streetlight on every corner. No signs of the hustle and bustle associated with places like

Columbia and Charleston, the two biggest cities in the state. Greenwood is located in the northwest section of South Carolina, and is not that far from the Georgia border.

To get to the church where Willie Bluford's funeral was held, the bus traveled down a long country road surrounded by what looked like a corn field. Eventually the bus came to a clearing and pulled up to the front entrance of a small building that's painted in a milky-white color. A cemetery was located on church grounds.

Inside, there was not a lot of pew space. At best, this church wasn't built to accommodate more than sixty people, and the members of the caravan occupied nearly every seat. With Bluford's family and friends in attendance, plus the people from Marshall, folks were lined up along the walls and there may have been even more people standing outside the front door. The space was tight, practically elbow-to-elbow.

Even though this was late November, this was still the Deep South where steamy temperatures are the norm, even at that time of year. There was no air conditioning, no ceiling fans, no floor fans. The sole source of relief: those trusty hand-held fans that worked overtime on that day.

The rustic setting in Greenwood was reminiscent of the past, a time in which previous generations of black people made their livelihood off the land as farmers or sharecroppers.

After Bluford's homegoing on Sunday, a weary troupe of travelers headed home to Marshall late that afternoon and arrived back on campus some time after midnight. The job of saying farewell was completed and it was good to be back in familiar surroundings. This group shared so many highs and lows during this trip. And they harvested a lifetime's worth of memories that we now view as history.

Some went to class on Monday. Others slept for most of the day, knowing they would be leaving again in a few days to go on Thanksgiving break. More time to unwind, more time to reflect.

"Coming back, everyone was pretty much drained," Lawson Brooks explained. "But, we all came back with a greater sense of appreciation, not only for the guys who died, but better feelings for each other. By going on this trip, it made me value my life a lot more. It made me want to accomplish certain things, knowing that life is not promised, that it can all be gone in a moment."

For Angela Dodson, the caravan journey provided her with a viable means to deal with a great loss. "During that whole time, you kept thinking that this just couldn't be real," she said. "That trip gave all of us a way to honor the memory of those players in a way that took away that sense of helplessness. The act of going to all those funerals performed that function of doing something concrete, rather than sitting around on campus and hearing about everything later on."

*****

Honoring the memory of the deceased black football players did not stop when the caravan returned to campus. The quiet ripples of grief transformed into an unexpected wave of unity, hope, and remembrance. Imagine, if you will, a group of grieving college students, each carrying the weight of their lost friends on their shoulders. That burden could've easily crushed their spirits and left them broken. But instead, they rose. They found solace in art, in performances, in each other. What started as a simple church fellowship blossomed into something far more profound – the Soul Searchers of First Baptist in Huntington. Scottie Reese, the first president of the fellowship, was the engaging personality that led them.

Now, instead of only gathering in the comfort of fellowship, they took to the stage, their raw emotions channeled into art. With an improvised Broadway musical *Purlie,* the rhythmic heartbeats of dance, the poignant strokes of poetry, and the inspired singing of Gospel songs, they immortalized the memory of their departed peers. As Paulette (Dodson) Scott, one of the dancers, beautifully put it, "This became our way of telling our story." For these students, tragedy wasn't the end; it was a turning point.

Still, their story needed a larger stage, and thus, the Soul Searchers went on tour. First, the northern tour during the spring break of '71, touching hearts of audiences in Richmond, Virginia, New York City, Philadelphia, Boston, and Springfield, Massachusetts. It was a journey of not just music and dance, but of healing, of sharing their sorrow and hope with others.

Next, came the southern Reconciliation Tour in the summer, aiming to do more than remember those who perished. They wanted to pay homage, and convey a powerful message about unity among races. While sports can unite backgrounds, it was the weight of the tragedy, as Joe Bundy expressed, that solidified their connections. With performances in Bluefield, West Virginia, Jacksonville, Florida, and two stops in Texas –Dallas and Waco – they aimed to show the need for blacks and whites to coexist peacefully, especially during a time when racial tensions were close to reaching a boiling point in many parts of the country.

However, it was the visit to Waco that would etch itself into the memories of the Soul Searchers the most. When the group set foot on the ground of Paul Quinn College, emotions swelled. For here was Scottie's hometown and, heartbreakingly, his final resting place.

Tears flowed as they performed, a blend of sorrow for the life lost and joy for the legacy continued. Bill Redd, the group's drummer, recounted the profound connection they felt when meeting Scottie's father, Chester. The sheer gratitude in the elder Reese's eyes, knowing his son had touched so many lives, was overwhelming. "It was a healing experience for him and for us," Bill reflected. Scottie's tragic end wasn't just a personal loss for his family; it was a collective heartbreak shared by all who knew him.

The plane crash was a moment in time that could've shattered bonds and squashed spirits. Yet, for the Soul Searchers and many black students at Marshall, it did the opposite. It forged a robust bond that's just as powerful today as it was in those initial days and months after the disaster. The Soul Searchers turned their heartbreak into an ongoing symphony of hope and memory.

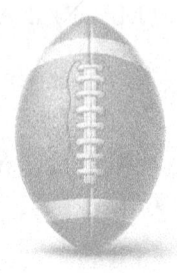

CHAPTER SIX

Forever Embedded

The weight of the plane crash pressed down on the students of Marshall like a thousand-pound anchor. Imagine the life of these young souls for a moment. One day, they were joking around with friends in the hallway, discussing plans for the weekend, and the next, they were attending funerals, trying to make sense of a world suddenly plunged into chaos. It was as if the universe had played a cruel joke on Marshall.

In their midst, familiar faces vanished — the ones they used to nod to in the library corridors and laugh with during impromptu meet-ups at the student union. These were the people they had imagined sharing future successes and failures with, embarking on adventures, and celebrating milestones. Those departed had dreams and aspirations just like them, doodling plans in their notebooks, discussing future endeavors, and setting goals. Now, it wasn't just the present they mourned; it was the infinite tomorrows that were tragically snatched away.

Consider the depth of the void for those who had even closer ties. The lady who had dreams of a future wedding with her Marshall beau, the student who had grown up sharing everything with a buddy since childhood, only to lose them in an unforeseen tragedy. Or the roommates who'd made promises of global escapades after graduation.

But what if that plane had never met its terrible fate? Those bonds, those shared hopes and dreams, would have most likely transformed into tales told in their golden years, shared over family get-togethers, reminiscing about their spirited days at Marshall. A haunting "what could have been" will forever linger in their minds. Delve into their world, and listen to their stories.

*****

The last time Macie Lugo saw Larry "Dupree" Sanders was the day before the crash – in "the pit," a sunken lounge area in Twin Towers girls' dorm. The pit was a haven for couples to savor quiet moments amidst the busy pace of college life. Soft, subdued lighting bathed the room, making the ambiance even more romantic. It was here that Macie and Dupree shared one of their final moments.

When Dupree left town that day, a small token made its mark in Macie's memory—a dime on the carpet. Although uncertain, she felt it might have slipped from Dupree's pocket. That dime, inconspicuous as it might be to others, became a poignant reminder of Larry Sanders for Macie. "It was his way of letting me know that he's always watching out for me," she said.

November 1970 promised warmth and cheer with the approaching Thanksgiving holiday. Macie had hoped to introduce Dupree to her family in Bluefield, West Virginia. When he dithered about visiting, hinting at possibly going home to Alabama, Macie was disappointed. Back then, a boyfriend visiting a girlfriend's home during the holidays indicated a committed relationship. And everyone knew Dupree and Macie were a "serious" couple.

Fate, however, had a different plan. Macie found herself in Alabama, not for a festive holiday feast, but for a somber funeral. The weight of the situation was heavy on her heart, not just for the loss of her boyfriend, but also for the families of Robert VanHorn, Freddy Wilson, and Joe Hood. She empathized deeply, reflecting, "All I could think about was how great a loss it was. It was so sad, for me and for the families."

It was in Alabama that Macie encountered a surprise that tugged at her heartstrings. A private conversation with one of Dupree's relatives revealed a secret he'd held close. He'd decided to spend Thanksgiving with her in Bluefield, and had intentionally kept Macie in the dark, probably relishing the thought of surprising her. A tearful Macie confessed, "I didn't have any idea until I was there for his funeral."

The return trip to West Virginia was agonizing. Macie, accompanied by her friend Murrial, found themselves in Atlanta for a layover. As they waited, familiar faces emerged from the concourse. It was Dupree's oldest brother and his wife, residents of Atlanta, which was unbeknownst to Macie. The breakthrough moment came when Dupree's sister-in-law warmly embraced Macie. With that hug, the weight of grief was momentarily lifted. Macie felt acknowledged, comforted, and understood. That single gesture spoke volumes, reflecting the deep connections people can make in times of sorrow. "What a gift that was," Macie recalled. "She felt my personal struggle and pain and she comforted me."

A few weeks after the plane crash, Macie finally felt like she could start sharing her innermost thoughts. But instead of some warmth or even just a simple "I'm here for you," what did she get? *"It's about time that we moved on from that (plane crash),"* she was told. I mean, who says that? And here's the most shocking part. This cold, heartless statement came from a trusted ally. Macie wouldn't even reveal the person's name.

With all her history of always being there for others, comforting, taking care, you'd imagine there'd be a line of people waiting to hold her up. But nope, nothing. It's as if everyone around her just went mute, forgetting she had feelings too. With such harsh words still echoing in her head, she made this resolve, *"Fine, I'll bottle it all up and power through."* She just retreated deeper into herself. But wait, it doesn't end there. Her dad, of all people, had some downright bizarre viewpoints about Macie's state of mind.

Macie, draped in her grief, had taken to wearing a lot of black in her wardrobe. Earl Lugo, in all his supposed wisdom, offered up this biting remark. "You need to stop wearing so much black. You are not a widow." Can you fathom that? And this coming from a man who literally dealt with death as his day job (mortician). It's absolutely mind-blowing. OK, I understand wanting your child to heal, but really? Macie must've been thinking, *"Is everyone expecting me to just snap out of it like it's some bad dream?"*

This whole episode taught Macie something profound. Grief isn't a one-size-fits-all hat. Every individual has their own way, their own pace. And she believes that if someone doesn't allow that natural grieving process to take place, they're setting themselves up for some serious emotional pitfalls. By her own admission, Macie made a few choices she's not proud of. Relationships, career moves, she reckons she's lost some fantastic chances because she didn't truly process her pain.

Quite honestly, it's gut-wrenching. Those final months in school? Macie described them as nothing short of a "prolonged death march." It's like every day was this endless loop of hurt, longing, and an overwhelming sense of loss. Life was now dramatically different. Understandably, she had difficulties seeing past her grief. To keep her mind occupied, she buried herself in her books. As for any semblance of a social life? Forget it.

But then, Reggie Oliver happened. He lost four close friends in the crash, including Larry Sanders. Yet, despite his pain, he had this deep-seated urge to make sure Macie didn't spiral into becoming a full-time recluse. The Twin Towers dorm had become her self-made prison, and it was quite startling for her when Reggie started knocking on her door every weekend. And, get this, he wasn't alone. He brought along his date, attempting to form a sort of makeshift trio for outings.

"Reggie wasn't going to let me sit around the dorm every weekend," Macie recalls. "Imagine this: Me, someone neck-deep in grief, going out with a buddy and his lady who probably thought she had this exclusive date with the star quarterback. Suddenly, she's part of this... emotional threesome." Reggie Oliver genuinely believed that without a nudge, Macie might never step out. Having won the Miss Black Pearl pageant to reign as the school's black homecoming queen, she was a notable figure at Marshall. So, it was heartbreaking to see her turn into a shadow. Oliver once mentioned, "There was this gap in people's lives after the crash. We were all walking wounded. So, I thought, why not help create a sense of normalcy?"

When the spring of '71 rolled in, Reggie had that big Varsity-Alumni game to play in. Obviously, he couldn't be Macie's chaperone for that one. And while many thought Macie would skip it, given the fresh scars, she showed up. "I wanted to show my support for the guys carrying on," she told me. While she was keen to uplift the players, it became clear that she herself needed encouragement. As things turned out, that was the last time Macie watched a Marshall football game in person. But don't get it twisted. The crash didn't make her turn away from sports. She kept tabs on the Herd through TV and newspapers.

After wrapping up her sophomore year at Marshall, Macie mulled over whether to stick around. She even toyed with the idea of diving into the vibrant world of Howard University in Washington, DC. But all plans fell by the wayside when her dad made a difficult-to-decline offer during the summer of '71. If she chipped in at the family's funeral home business and watched over her kid sisters, he'd foot the entire college bill. How could she say no?

Macie packed her bags and made her way to Bluefield State College, eventually graduating in '72 with a degree in teacher's education. So, what prompted the switch? After the crash that took Dupree, things were just... different. The good ol' friends they used to hang out with? The dynamics shifted. Some folks tiptoed around her, lost for words, not knowing how to bridge that gaping chasm of grief. "Nothing was ever the same," she lamented. "It was time to move on. I needed to be in another environment."

Though Macie left Marshall and graduated elsewhere, she later settled in Dunbar, West Virginia, just 50 miles away. Fate had its way, and she became well-acquainted with the roads to Huntington. Every visit had its own meaning, and none of them were related to the nostalgic allure of homecoming. Her motivation was her nephew, Mark. His bright eyes, which sometimes found the world a bit too overwhelming due to his autism, had a special place in her heart.

The West Virginia Autism Training Center, housed on the MU campus, was Mark's second home. This center had been his sanctuary, a place of solace, understanding and learning. And every time Macie visited, her heart swelled with pride to see how Mark was progressing.

On each visit, the path Macie took always led her past the Memorial Student Union. And right there, standing tall and elegant, was the Memorial Fountain. Crafted in '72, this tulip-shaped marvel wasn't just for aesthetic appeal. It bore the weight of memories, the heartache of loss, and the hope for renewal. Those seventy-five points atop? Each one was a silent scream, a story, a face, and a name. The souls of the passengers of that horrific flight were immortalized through it.

The changing seasons added a poetic touch to the fountain's tale. Come spring, its waters danced freely, celebrating life and all its wonders. But in the chill of winter, it stood still, making one remember the cold reality of that fateful night from many years ago. During those visits, the stillness of the fountain always greeted Macie. It mirrored the somber notes in her heart. "Walking by it without the water flowing, it felt as if time froze," she said. "But what truly warms my heart is that every year, without fail, the community remembers. They never forget, and that's very special."

So, while Macie's visits were primarily for Mark, the campus and its stories always tugged at her heartstrings. She might not have returned for the revelries of homecoming, but the spirit, history, and memories of Marshall were forever embedded in her soul. The bonds she formed there, the lessons she learned, and the struggles she dealt with, equipped her with a depth of understanding that went beyond textbooks and lecture halls. These very experiences made her an emblem of resilience, a beacon of hope for those who faced adversity.

In a parallel universe not so far from Macie's home, the Charleston High School gym echoed with triumphs of its own. Every bounce of the ball, every squeak of the sneaker, told tales of past glories. But the freshmen and sophomores of the basketball team, sitting dejectedly in an anatomy class on an unassuming day, were unfamiliar with the sting of defeat. Until recently, that is.

They were supposed to be out witnessing history, the presidential inauguration of Barack Obama. But a shortage of buses and a stroke of luck for others left them behind. Their disappointment was palpable. They wore their frustration outwardly, not only about missing out on the DC trip, but also about their sudden losing streak on the court. Enter Macie, the substitute teacher for the day. A juxtaposition of grace and strength, with her history painted with challenges after a personal tragedy. Most would see a classroom filled with despondent teenagers. But Macie? She saw an opportunity to bridge the lessons of her life to theirs.

She didn't start with a pep talk about basketball strategies or about revisiting their game techniques. Instead, she delved deep, connecting basketball to life, drawing parallels, and using it as an allegory for the greater game they were all playing.

"Sports has always been my way to connect with guys like you," she said, her voice warm and inviting. "Listen to me. Your outside shot could be beyond the NBA three-point line and you could be Stevie Wonder and still make the shot," she explained, sparking a few amused glances among the students. "You could be an Honor Roll student and be dating the school's homecoming queen. You can have all the Kobe (Bryant) and LeBron (James) game jerseys and travel places to see your favorite pro teams play. These are signs that life is good."

Then she paused, letting the words sink in, her gaze capturing each student's. "But that's not the time when the most beneficial information comes. It comes when you're losing, when you're faced with adverse circumstances. Those are the situations that define your character. It gives you strength and perseverance. The life lessons come from loss and from loneliness and despair. Those are the situations that help prepare you for the life you're going to have. When everything is joyous and free, the lessons don't come from that place. *They come from the other place.*"

The room was thick with an electrified silence. Every eye was on her, every ear tuned in, absorbing her wisdom, understanding that this was more than just about a game. "Maaannnnn!" an impressed basketball player exclaimed, breaking the silence. "We like you. When are you coming back again?"

Macie, in her wisdom, used that one day, that one "'substitute" moment, to change perspectives, and potentially, the trajectory of the lives in that room. She demonstrated that sometimes, the game of life is played best not when you're winning, but when you're learning from your losses.

* * * *

Janice Cooley was swept up in a budding romance with Art Harris, one of the Herd's star running backs. They had begun dating in September '70, and life seemed radiant. But as the leaves transitioned into their fiery hues, a peculiar shadow fell over Artie. What was once an upbeat demeanor turned somber, with Artie speaking frequently of mortality. "That's all he would talk about," Janice recalled. "He kept asking me over and over and over again: 'What you would do if I were to die?'"

For Janice, an eighteen-year-old college freshman, the conversation felt out of place. She was just getting started with her adult life; why would death be on the agenda? Yet, her love for Artie compelled her to reply, "Artie, if you died, I'd want to die too." It was a response born more from the heart's longing to comfort than from any dark contemplation.

One evening, a drive in Artie's white 1966 Pontiac Bonneville created another opportunity for him to broach the subject. "Artie and I were driving around outside of Huntington and he noticed three crosses at the top of a hill near the highway," Janice said. The sight seemed to draw Artie in, and once more, they (Harris, Janice and a couple of football players who rode in the back seat) found themselves in a conversation about life's end. But Artie's preoccupation didn't end there. Quite unexpectedly, he asked Janice to accompany him to church. "The invitation to Sunday morning worship service at First Baptist took me by surprise," she admitted, "especially since Artie wasn't a regular there."

Days moved on, revealing yet more unexpected facets of Artie. One evening, sitting outside in his parked car, they talked deeply before deciding to drive over to a friend's house where Artie would make a phone call. He dialed a long-distance number to Passaic, New Jersey from his friend's place. On the other end was his mother, and after their conversation, he handed the phone to Janice. After that call, Artie opened up about his life in New Jersey – from being a single father to giving the skinny on his family and even the neighborhood dogs.

The day before the crash remains hauntingly vivid for Janice. As Artie and Janice walked over to the gym, she recalls their long embrace, punctuated by a parting kiss. Yet, what weighed on her heart the most were Artie's departing words: *"If I don't come back, tell my mom to give my clothes away. And I want you to keep my car."* The next day, the world changed forever. Artie was gone, leaving behind a void and a bewildering sense of premonition. Reflecting on everything, Janice said, "After all this time, that's the one thing that keeps sticking with me. It was like he knew he was going to die."

On the night of November 14, Janice's world shattered. Her heartbreak was so profound that she had to be whisked away to a nearby hospital. The sterile scent of her surroundings and the cool needle prick of the doctor's shot meant to calm her frazzled nerves, provided little solace. Each beat of her heart echoed with loss, reverberating with the agonizing question: "Why? Why Artie?" As she grappled with her devastating reality, relief came in the form of familiar voices. Viola and Paul, her parents, had driven three hours on a moment's notice to be there for their daughter, to try and piece together her broken heart.

The following day ushered in a fresh wave of anguish. Driven by an inexplicable urge, Janice found herself standing outside Artie's room at the South Hall dorm. The door opened and there stood Felix Jordan, Artie's roommate. His gaunt face and red eyes spoke of a pain that mirrored Janice's. He, too, was tormented by the harrowing images of the previous night's horror. Once inside Artie's room, Janice was surrounded by memories of him – the warmth, the familiarity, and the deafening silence that confirmed his absence. She laid on his bed, letting her tears stain the fabric, seeking some semblance of connection to him.

As she left the room, a crushing revelation awaited her. Artie's father had been aboard that ill-fated plane. Memories of their brief meeting earlier in the season flooded her mind. The weight of the tragedy bore down on her even more as she considered Mia Wagner Harris, now bereft of her husband and son. A family shattered, with only a grieving mother and two sisters left to pick up the pieces.

Fate, however, had yet another twist in store. Janice later found out about a chilling premonition that cast a dark shadow a few hours before the tragedy. Earlier that day, during a routine call home, Janice's grandmother, Gertrude Green, had felt an ominous uneasiness while talking to her granddaughter. After ending the call with Janice, she confided in Janice's mother about her foreboding feeling, saying, "Something is going to happen—not good." It was as if Gertrude had eerily sensed the looming catastrophe. "My grandmother always *felt* things," Janice declared.

The heaviness of those days, the tidal wave of sorrow Janice experienced was palpable. While it's difficult to adequately explain such profound pain and loss, anyone who has loved deeply and faced such loss might understand a sliver of Janice's heartache. Walking into a room full of strangers and yet, in the midst of all those unknown faces, recognizing them from Artie's loving descriptions, was nothing short of surreal. Each time Janice looked into the eyes of a relative or a friend, she felt as though she was gazing upon a piece of Artie, his life and legacy intertwined with every handshake and every tear shed.

For Janice, the intensity of that joint funeral service was a labyrinth of emotions. From her vantage point, every detail—whether it was the soft sobbing in the background, the solemn whispers exchanged between Artie's friends, or the simple act of driving Artie's car back to New Jersey—felt magnified. His mother's embrace was a gesture filled with shared pain and mutual understanding, offering Janice a temporary shelter from the storm of grief surrounding them. In that tight embrace, Mrs. Harris' grip conveyed more than words ever could. They became two souls united by a single, tragic thread.

Returning to college was like stepping into a different world, a version of reality where shadows of Artie lurked around every corner. Every classroom, every hallway was a stark reminder of the gaping void left by his absence. The sight of jersey No. 22 wasn't just a number; it was a symbol of the love they shared and the heartbreak of its abrupt ending. The very air seemed saturated with memories. Spending weekends in nearby Charleston offered a brief reprieve, a chance to escape and pretend, even if just for a moment, that the tragedy hadn't eclipsed her world. Yet, deep down, she knew she couldn't run forever. Gradually, Janice mustered the strength to face her memories head-on and inch her way towards a feeling of stability.

The bond with Artie's family remained through the late '70s. Janice worked in New York City, so it was no problem to travel to New

Jersey. But with every visit, the sorrow was rekindled. Mrs. Harris' tears spoke of a pain that seemed insurmountable, a hurt so profound that Janice began to question if her presence was more of a torment than a solace. That's when she made the agonizing decision to distance herself, hoping it might ease Mrs. Harris' burden.

Fast forward to 2004.

In a sleek corporate office, sunlight streamed through the blinds, casting bars of light on the polished table. But the room's focus was the delicate dance unfolding between two individuals. Janice, with her professional demeanor, sat confidently behind her desk, looking intently at the job candidate across from her. This was a typical job interview setting, where skills are assessed and futures are decided. However, today's interview was about to take a deeply personal detour.

One detail on the candidate's resume stood out, acting as a portal to Janice's past: the University of Virginia. The mere mention of it stirred old memories, compelling her to delve deeper. She ventured, "Hmmm, Virginia. You know I'm from West Virginia," her tone suggesting more than casual curiosity.

The job candidate leaned in, clearly interested in where this was heading. "Yes, I'm familiar with West Virginia," he replied measuredly. "I almost went to college there."

A spark of intrigue lit up Janice's eyes. "Which college were you considering,?" she asked, her professional demeanor momentarily overshadowed by personal interest.

Picking up on her tone, he answered with a touch of nostalgia, "Marshall University."

"Interesting," Janice said, emotions threatening to spill. "I'm a Marshall graduate."

His eyes widened in surprise. "What a coincidence. My best friend in high school went to Marshall. Tragically, he was in that plane crash."

Trying to steady her voice, Janice gently inquired, "Who was your best friend?"

"Artie Harris," he shared, voice laden with wistfulness.

Overwhelmed and initially speechless, Janice's world momentarily pauses. In her mind's eye, she's transported back to those blissful college days at Marshall. She recalls laughter-filled walks, her hand in Artie's hand. They're young, in love, their futures a canvas of endless possibilities.

Even now Janice marvels at how this surprising chain of events played out. "It was just unbelievable that I was sitting there talking to this guy," she said. "He knew all about the family. And he knew *everything* about Artie."

And so, in a setting designed for professional assessments, two souls connected over a shared past and the poignant memories of a dear friend. It was a powerful reminder that life's narratives can intersect in the most unexpected places.

* * * * *

About a month before the crash, Debbie (Bailey) Bowen broke up with Bobby Hill, who played cornerback for the Herd. But this isn't just a story about lost love. No, this story hits deeper. You see, Debbie was a trailblazer. She had the honor and challenge of being the first black cheerleader at Marshall. Now, for some, that might have been intimidating. But not for Debbie. And she wasn't alone. Enter Freddy Wilson, Joe Hood, and Robert VanHorn – the 'Bama guys. They practically adopted Debbie. "They treated me like I was their baby sister," she fondly remembered.

VanHorn had that big brother vibe that everyone craves. After catching wind of Debbie's breakup, he took her aside and said with all the warmth and concern of an elder sibling, "You're going to meet Mr. Right, just hang in there." Debbie's eyes would twinkle as she remembered, "The talk we had really helped."

And then there was Wilson. He wasn't just any guy on campus – he was one of the few black dudes cruising around in his own car. Every day, after Debbie was done with cheerleading practice, she'd chill at the Twin Towers cafeteria and wait on Freddy. Once Freddy got in from football practice and grabbed some grub, he would drive Debbie home. Every. Single. Day. Rain or shine. "He never even asked for gas money," Debbie said. The bond was so deep that Freddy once popped a question that caught Debbie completely off guard. "Why don't you come home with us for Thanksgiving? Trust me, it's going to be a ton of fun!"

Debbie laughed, "You really think my daddy's gonna let me go on a road trip with three guys? All the way to Alabama? But, you know, if you come over for dinner and ask him, he just might." Debbie's dad was Max Bailey, one of Marshall's biggest football aficionados. After a Sunday dinner where Wilson, VanHorn, and Hood put on their most charming smiles and assured Mr. Bailey of their intentions, he gave his approval. Debbie was headed to Alabama!

But fate had other plans. What was supposed to be a Thanksgiving trip turned into a journey of heartbreak. "The trip to Alabama felt endless," Debbie whispered, her voice breaking. "I was so depressed, all I did was sleep."

Debbie always reminisced about those 'Bama guys with such warmth, thinking of how they had her back when she took the leap to try out for Marshall's cheerleading squad. Every black player for the Herd rooted for her, but those Tuscaloosa fellas? They were in a league of their own when it came to vocal support. Debbie remembered thinking, *"If our teams are diverse, why shouldn't our cheerleaders reflect that too?"* She later found out those three – Wilson, Hood, and VanHorn – weren't just being vocal. They took it a step further. They'd told the school straight-up: "No black cheerleaders? Well, then maybe you don't get players."

Debbie felt those Alabama guys really knew how to stand their ground. Growing up in the Deep South during the height of the civil rights era had given them a backbone like no other. "They realized the power of taking a stand," she said with admiration. "They were ready to risk their scholarships just to do what was right. The more years that pass, the more it hits me – the weight of what they did."

And while they never dived deep into heart-to-heart chats about Debbie breaking the color barrier as a cheerleader, there was this hilarious moment she'll never forget. After one game, VanHorn, with a twinkle in his eye, said, "It was pretty refreshing seeing those black legs kicking high on the sidelines." Chuckling, Debbie shot back, "Real smooth, guys. Appreciate it."

"They noticed me," Debbie said. "They felt pride, but they sure had a comical way of showing it."

Flashback to the spring of '70: A resolute group of black students, with fire in their eyes and courage in their hearts, meet with MU administrators. Their plea? Let blacks cheer alongside their white counterparts. But the answer they received was layered in prejudice, with undertones of bigotry. "Marshall isn't ready for black cheerleaders," they were told, as if color dictated spirit or enthusiasm.

Now, here's where the narrative takes a twist. Refusing to back down, black student leaders devised a strategy to ensure that blacks got a genuine opportunity to make the squad. Like a chess master anticipating the opponent's moves, these leaders offered a solution. Give the hopeful black cheerleaders a training ground, a chance to sharpen their skills alongside the existing cheerleaders of Marshall.

Enter Debbie, who was not the quintessential cheerleader one would picture. No, her arena had always been the long jump and high jump pits, where she soared through the air in defiance of gravity. Organized sports for women during her time? Almost unheard of! Yet, in a meeting with destiny, Howard Henderson, one of the student leaders, approached her and Toni Brown with an unexpected proposal: train to be a Marshall cheerleader..

Toni and Debbie, novices to the cheering world, quickly discovered the gravity of what they had taken on. The athleticism, agility, and grace required for cheerleading were on a completely different spectrum from anything they had ever experienced. Think about it: two young women, throwing their bodies into new motions, feeling the burn of unused muscles, and pushing through the physical challenges. Yet, amidst the hurdles, Debbie recalls a heartwarming silver lining.

The Marshall cheerleaders, contrary to her expectations, welcomed them with open arms. No sneers, no disdainful glances. Just pure camaraderie. They laughed, they trained, and they prepared for the big day together. Debbie's voice, dripping with nostalgia, echoes the sentiment: "I'll never forget their kindness."

The genuine warmth of the Marshall cheerleaders was a surprising comfort for Debbie. Yet, behind that gratitude lay the deeper pain of the plane crash. Imagine bearing an iron weight in your chest for 39 long years. An iron so heavy and unyielding, it overshadows every facet of your life, casting its formidable presence over every decision, every emotion. That was Debbie. A proud graduate of Marshall, a zesty cheerleader who once took center stage, shaking her pom-poms to the rhythm of the roaring crowd, the embodiment of school spirit. But then, life dealt a cruel blow. The crash. It was more than a tragic event. It stole her own spirit. The lady who once stood at the forefront cheering for Marshall retreated, disappearing into the shadows of grief and melancholy.

Fast forward to the 2009 homecoming game. I mean, really put yourself in her shoes. Can you feel the emerald grass beneath your feet? The energy in the stadium, it's so palpable, like a living entity all on its own. But for Debbie, stepping into Edwards Stadium wasn't just about the game. It was like opening an old, dusty book, its pages yellowed with time, each one holding a memory, a moment, a tear.

Seeing her fellow cheerleaders from '70, it was like looking into a mirror reflecting a past version of herself. They had all changed, of course. Lines of time marking their faces, but their eyes? Oh, those eyes held the same pain, the same memories. And as the introductions rolled in, it was a whirlwind of emotions. The young college days, the laughs, the hopes, everything came flooding back.

Now, I want you to picture this - the massive video screen lighting up, displaying *that photo*. Not just any photo. It was their youth, their innocence, frozen in time, preserved forever. Them, in their prime, running down the ramp. It wasn't just a reminder of the past; it was a tribute, an ode to their spirit, their resilience. The applause that followed was deafening. Not the kind you give when your team scores a touchdown, but the kind that comes straight from the heart. It resonated and it echoed, filling the stadium, and perhaps every crevice of Debbie's heart.

Running with the current cheerleaders, she wasn't just reliving her youth. It was her reclaiming her place, her identity. She wasn't the lady left behind anymore. She was a part of something bigger, a legacy, a memory that would live on. Later, reflecting on that day,

Debbie would realize the profound shift within her. That standing ovation wasn't just for them. It was for the strength they symbolized, for every tear they had shed, for every smile they had lost, and every moment they had missed.

Is that closure, or what? Oh, it was sweet. Imagine 39 years of anguish melting away, replaced with a sense of belonging, recognition, and most importantly, love. For Debbie, that homecoming wasn't just a game; it was a moment of rebirth, a beacon of hope, signaling the start of a brand new chapter. Man, life throws curveballs, doesn't it? But sometimes, just sometimes, it gives you a moment so profound, it changes everything. And for Debbie, Homecoming 2009 was just that.

"I won't ever forget that day," she said with a beaming smile. "When I saw that picture on the big screen, it was closure for me after all those years. After that, I was OK."

* * * * *

Whenever Reggie Oliver went home to Tuscaloosa, Alabama, he always made it a point to visit Cedar Oak Memorial Park. But it's not just family he visits. His friends Larry Sanders, Joe Hood, Robert VanHorn, and Freddy Wilson rest there too. "I always stop by to chat with the fellas," he said. "They get the latest updates from me on what's happening at Marshall. I always feel their presence."

That dark night of the crash always haunted Reggie. Imagine him, just coming back from a store run, and then - the news. Panic, disbelief, a need to be at the scene. "All I could think about was getting to the airport," he recalled. Picture a car filled with anxious MU athletes arriving at the scene, navigating through heavy underbrush, and following an unpaved road to the unimaginable. The unforgettable scent of burning jet fuel, mingled with thick smoke, lingered in the air. They stood just 400 yards away from the charred site, unable to get any closer as the area had been cordoned off by rescue workers. Among the departed were those four guys from Tuscaloosa. "To stand and watch as I did out at the airport that night was very difficult. The smoke was so thick, I could smell it in my clothes," Reggie recounted with a heavy heart.

Now, let's not forget, Tuscaloosa had a budding legacy at Marshall. Sanders paved the way in '68, and a year later, Hood, VanHorn, Wilson, Flozell Horton, and Coach Kenneth O'Rourke joined the Herd. Reggie, the youngest of the Tuscaloosa pack, came in '70. Life took its turns with Horton bowing out due to injury and O'Rourke shifting career paths. But through it all, Reggie persevered. "The terror of the tragedy is forever inescapable," he said. "But I do not dwell on that. The memories I have of the '70 team are good ones."

But here's the thing: Reggie had a tangible piece of that past. A ring, one meant for a player from the '70 team, Tom Brown. Since the intended recipients all died in the crash, those rings were not presented until a few years after the crash. Coach Jack Lengyel gave the rings to members of the Young Thundering Herd who came onboard in '71 and stuck it out until the end of their senior seasons. Reggie wore the ring practically every day. Why? "I've received rings when Marshall won two national championships," he said, "But that ring from '70 is very special. It's a constant reminder."

For Reggie Oliver, that ring represents a bond, a vow, a commitment to always remember and uphold the legacy of the '70 team. Reggie's legacy and that ring continue to inspire generations about unity, perseverance, and the echoes of history. When Oliver arrived at Marshall, there was a spark in his eye and a mission in his heart. Alongside him, his five inseparable buddies from back home shared a dream - a vision so vivid, it seemed like you could grasp it from the air. They weren't just there to play; they were there to ignite a revolution, to rewrite the history of Marshall.

Whispered tales among the Herd's most ardent fans tell of those lost in the tragic plane crash, suggesting they never truly left. They say these spirits linger, silently cheering, aiding, and intervening on behalf of Marshall. It's the Herd's mystical "twelfth man" - a presence that's not just the stuff of legends but felt profoundly by many.

Recall the Marshall miracle against Xavier in '71? Those who were present will never forget. It was as if an unseen force was pushing the Young Thundering Herd beyond its limits. Even if you're a skeptic, one glance at the figures and you'd sense there's something exceptional going on here. Edwards Stadium (fondly known as "the Joan") threw open its gates in '91 and Marshall's game has ascended to astronomical heights.

Just take a moment to soak in this staggering stat: Marshall boasts a home winning percentage of .808 (entering the 2024 season). For those who swear by numbers, this feat, highlighted by Wikipedia, is among the elite in major-college football. Over the span of 32 thrilling seasons at "the Joan," the Herd rang up an impressive 182 wins with only forty-three losses. This fuels the notion that there's an undeniable force which continues to make hearts thunder with pride.

"If you believe and have faith, you believe in the unseen," Oliver declared. "When you look at what's happened with Marshall year by year after the crash, there's no way to explain it other than the existence of the twelfth man. The twelfth man has been present and will be ever present at Marshall University. Teams don't know what they're getting into when they play Marshall. They're not just playing against eleven people on the field. They're playing against a force."

In hindsight, Reggie's perspective proved to be prophetic. I witnessed something extraordinary at Marshall's memorial game in 2023 (played in honor of the crash victims). As we faced Georgia Southern, the weight of a five-game losing streak loomed large. But in the game's final, breathless minutes, with Marshall up 31-26, the impossible unfolded in front of an anxious home crowd. On one drive, the Herd miraculously recovered two of its own fumbles. It felt like a force beyond the field was at play. Then, John McConnell delivered a 42-yard punt that inexplicably stopped at the 2-yard line, defying every law of physics. The air was electric with disbelief and hope. We held Georgia Southern in their tracks and quickly scored another touchdown to seal a 38-33 victory. This wasn't just a win; this was a moment of redemption, a powerful tribute to the enduring spirit of the 75 who perished. In every cheer, every play, and heart-stopping moment, their presence was deeply felt, transforming a regular football game into an extraordinary celebration of faith, tenacity and resilience.

*****

Larry "Ice Man" Isom always had a sixth sense for things, a knack for feeling the pulse of any situation. When it came to the football team's road trip to East Carolina, a nagging uneasiness settled in his core. "I had this gut feeling it would be a bad weekend, you know?," Isom said with a grimace. "I tried tipping off a few of the guys. They didn't say anything back, but what could they really do? They had a game. They had to be on board that plane."

The atmosphere in Isom's room that Thursday night before the crash was electric – it always was. A makeshift barbershop emerged, with the gentle buzz of clippers punctuating the laughter. Although he didn't moonlight as a barber regularly, when Bobby Hill, Scottie Reese, and Dennis Blevins wanted their Afros tuned up, Isom was the man to do it. His dorm room was *the* place to be. The faint flicker from a black-and-white TV, combined with the rhythmic beats of legends like Funkadelic and James Brown – made it a hotspot.

Bobby "Bee-Bop" Hill was Isom's main man. From their freshman days, their bond was evident. Known for his prominent Afro and striking gold-capped tooth, "Bee-Bop" had an unassuming appearance. However, on the field, his gamesmanship was undeniable. Isom often thought back to how Bee-Bop would run, almost as if propelled by the wind, especially when he ran close to 21-seconds flat in a 200-meter race at an intramural track meet. Amazing, when you consider he wasn't even in peak track form.

For Isom, the whole trip to Dallas for Bobby's funeral was like trying to remember a dream. Everything's hazy. He recalled the heart-wrenching sadness of the service and the embrace of Bobby's people. "What I remember more than anything is sitting in the front row," Isom said. "They treated me like family."

The week following the crash felt like an unending nightmare for Isom. His room, once filled with laughter and camaraderie, echoed with silence. But what haunted Isom more was the palpable presence he felt in his room at night. "I can't even begin to describe it," he said, his voice shaking slightly. "I'd wake up and feel someone above me.

It freaked me out, but I swear it was Bobby. I could just feel him. I ended up sleeping with the lights on for four or five nights in a row."

As the school year continued, the trauma of it all hit hard and Isom's academics took a nosedive. But gradually, the "Ice Man" bounced back, digging deep, pulling through with his degree in hand. Looking back, Isom's voice turned contemplative. "Those college days, man, they taught me the real value of life. Those of us who made it out of that dark time at Marshall, we carry the memories of those who didn't. We owe it to them, and to ourselves, to cherish every moment we have."

A sigh. A pause. "You know, we really are the lucky ones."

CHAPTER SEVEN

Rescued from the Brink

There's a saying: "Every story has two sides." But the tale of the Marshall plane crash is a veritable prism, casting light in a myriad of directions. Picture a giant jigsaw puzzle, each piece a portion of the truth, but some pieces—vital ones—are nowhere to be found. Now, I don't pretend to have all the answers. Heck, not one news outlet could possibly piece together every fragment of this intricate puzzle. But here's the rub: Ed Carter, Felix Jordan, and Dickie Carter (and no, he's not kin to Ed) aren't just any pieces of the puzzle; they're the corners, the anchors. Dive in with me, as we uncover their hidden truths and bring clarity to the tragedy and its aftermath.

*****

After pushing through another rigorous practice, Ed Carter made his way back to his dorm, every muscle voicing its fatigue. He was on the cusp of retreating into the solitude of his room when the distinct ring of the pay phone in the hallway arrested his steps. Picking up the receiver, he was met with his mother's voice, resonating all the way from Wichita Falls, Texas. It was a tone he'd never heard before - urgent and heavy. "Ed," she began, each word laden with grief, "your father is gone." The sorrow was overwhelming, but before he could fully process it, another chilling revelation from Sarah Word held him captive. "You must promise me you won't go to East Carolina," she said. "That plane will crash and there won't be anyone left."

Ed was stunned and puzzled.

"How could Mom know this and be so sure about it actually happening?," he thought. *"And how could she know about a plane trip that I didn't even know about? We always traveled by bus for away games."*

For Ed, the rock-solid offensive tackle, the thought of missing a game was alien. Yet, with the resonance of his mother's words and the weight of his father's departure pressing down on him, he played another home game, then made the somber journey to Texas. When the heart-wrenching news of the crash came through, the forewarning in his mother's voice echoed louder than ever. Ed was certain, beyond a shadow of a doubt, that this was God at work. That Divine message, draped in sorrow and prediction, had unquestionably saved his life. "In later discussions, my mom said that it was not a premonition when she told me about what would happen," Ed recalled. "She made it clear that God gave her that revelation as we talked."

After his father was laid to rest, Ed had sufficient time to make it back to West Virginia to rejoin the team for the East Carolina game. He had a roundtrip plane ticket, so he could have returned in time to get in two days of practice. In the meantime, Sarah kept insisting that Ed remain in Wichita Falls. "Every time she told me she didn't want me to go, she'd start crying," Ed remembers. "I didn't like seeing her cry, so I stayed home just to satisfy her."

The morning after the crash, Ed read about the disaster in the Sunday edition of the local paper, which erroneously listed him as one of the victims. "It was like reading my own obituary," he explained. Over the next few days, the phone never stopped ringing. Concerned friends and neighbors called to express their condolences. Ed answered some of the calls, which provided some much-needed relief for those who assumed that he was with the Marshall team. "After the crash," Ed said, "it didn't take much to persuade me to ride the bus back to West Virginia."

During the twenty-eight-hour bus ride back to Huntington, Ed could not escape the visual reminders of the tragedy. At every bus station, it seemed, every paper in the news racks featured front-page stories about the crash. The huge headlines in bold verified a chilling fact. Most of Ed's teammates died, but for some reason that was yet to be discovered, his life had been spared. Once Ed returned to West Virginia, he noticed a stark difference from what life was like before the tragedy and afterward. The somber mood of a city and campus in mourning was clearly evident. "It was like a ghost town almost," he said. "Everybody was down and depressed and discouraged. It was so disheartening."

There were some people who knew that Ed Carter was not on the plane. But this was not common knowledge to everyone. Ed discovered this after having a bizarre encounter with a schoolmate not long after he returned from Texas. Ida Franklin saw Ed and immediately did an about-face, walking so fast in the opposite direction that it seemed like she was getting ready to run. "Ida looked at me as if she had seen a ghost," Ed said. "I had to run to catch up with her. She had a hard time believing I was still alive. I explained what had happened and that helped her to calm down."

The November tragedy proved to be Ed's avenue for change in his personal life. Two months before his college graduation in 1974, he gave his life to Christ. That same year, he answered God's call to preach and started Death Unto Life Ministries, headquartered in Chattanooga, Tennessee. The foundation for Ed's ministry is rooted in his escape from the fatal plane crash. During its years of existence, Death Unto Life Ministries has touched hundreds of thousands in the United States and around the world.

"The Lord saved me to serve Him," Ed explained. "For all these years, I've been an unofficial ambassador for Marshall University. Everywhere I go, I tell people about how He saved me from the plane crash, saved my soul, and placed me in ministry. I've been given a variety of opportunities to reach people that I never would have reached, had it not been for the testimony that God has given me."

At speaking engagements, Ed Carter frequently displays a laminated copy of the story from his hometown newspaper that named him as one of the seventy-five passengers who were killed. That news article serves as a compelling visual tool. It helps Ed to effectively convey his message about God's intervention in rescuing him from a devastating plane crash.

Ten years into his soul-stirring sojourn as an evangelist, Ed was one of the headliners at a revival in Proctorville, Ohio, which is a stone's throw across the bridge from Huntington. As things turned out, this night became a memorable occasion for all the right reasons. Nate Ruffin, a Herd teammate for two seasons, showed up. And he wasn't just a curious audience member, he came with his entire family.

Now, the bond between Ed and Nate ran deep. Both were supposed to be on the plane, but they were no-shows. Ruffin was sidelined due to an injury and Ed was absent because of a death in the family. But most importantly, they shared the on-going agony of losing teammates in a fiery crash. Ed's sermon that night wasn't just any regular sermon. As he finished, a teary-eyed Nate, shaken to his core, ambled towards the altar. This was the night that Nate Ruffin surrendered his life to Christ.

Keep in mind, this was the same Nate who had heard Ed speak on numerous occasions. This time, things were different. It was as if the Lord himself spoke through Ed's words, gently pushing Nate towards salvation. Later, in the quiet confines of a pastor's office, Nate, a prominent business executive, spilled his heart out to Ed. Wiping away tears, he confided, "In spite of all my achievements, I feel... empty, like I've achieved nothing."

The following evening, the church was abuzz again, this time with "popcorn testimony." For the uninitiated, it's the segment of a service where folks spring up from their seats, like kernels in a microwave, to share what God has done in their lives. So, guess who popped up out of his seat, surprising even Ed? It was Nate! Freshly saved and not exactly versed in giving a testimony, Nate didn't care. He spoke from the depths of his soul and everybody in the audience knew it.

A decade earlier, Nate was one of the key figures who helped revive Marshall's football program, breathing life into it. But on this night, he spoke of a different kind of restoration, a personal one. For Ed, the image of Nate fervently giving his testimony is as vivid as ever. "I've been on the run from the Lord for years," Nate confessed to the congregation. "And I've heard Ed preach here and there. But last night ... God tackled me and I'm not running anymore."

Ruffin, who was later ordained as a deacon, served in a variety of capacities as an avid Marshall supporter. When the Herd played in its first NCAA Division I-AA national championship game in '87, he wasn't interested in watching it on television like most of the Marshall faithful. He wanted to be there in person. Getting there by air was out of the question. All flights were already booked. That's when he decided to hitchhike 1,844 miles from Huntington to Pocatello, Idaho, to attend that game.

Due to the time factor, driving his own car or traveling by bus or train was not a viable solution. By car, it would take at least two days of non-stop driving. But that would work *only* if there were enough passengers on hand to take turns driving, which would allow enough time for every driver to get sufficient rest. The schedules for buses and trains included so many stopovers, that the trip would take even longer than it would by car.

I can't say why Nate chose to hitchhike. But I do believe there was one compelling reason that fueled his desire to go to Idaho. When Marshall's freshman football team finished the season undefeated in '68, all of us on that team shared a collective vision. We were determined that by our senior year, Marshall would win a MAC championship and play in the Tangerine Bowl in Florida. We fell short of achieving our goal. But nineteen years later, *Marshall was playing for a national championship—in football.* This was the culmination of a vision that finally did come to pass. And the only way to fully bask in that experience was to physically be there in the stands, watching all the action as it unfolded.

Nate was heavily involved with several MU presidential search committees and was a member of the school's Alumni Board of Directors. In addition to his contributions as an athletics booster and recruiter, he was also active in Black Alumni of Marshall University. The Alumni Lounge in the Erickson Alumni Center on campus is named for Ruffin. Black Alumni secured the naming rights with a $100,000 pledge.

A granite cenotaph stands as a solemn tribute at the team's
memorial site at Spring Hill Cemetery in Huntington,
West Virginia. (Photo by Craig T. Greenlee)

Ruffin died of leukemia in 2001 and is buried at the memorial
site for the '70 team at Spring Hill Cemetery located on Huntington's
south side. A year prior to his passing away, Nate read an open letter
to his departed teammates that aired on the ABC TV network during
halftime of the 2000 MAC title game between Marshall and Western
Michigan. It was the thirtieth anniversary of the crash. (See "Nate
Ruffin" video on YouTube).

"For a while, I wished I was with you guys," Nate said in his letter. "But I realize now, many years later, that I was left here to keep your memory alive."

*****

By a stroke of destiny, Felix Jordan, the standout free safety, wasn't on that doomed flight. Imagine this: Felix, known as "X-Ray," was cozied up in his bus seat, eagerly waiting to head to the airport with his team. Then, out of the blue, a coach approached him, requesting his seat for an MU athletic booster who was chipping in for the cost of the flight. But that wasn't the sole reason for Felix's absence. The coaches believed that resting him for the ECU game would help his healing, so that he would be good to go for the climactic showdown against Ohio University the following week. Oddly enough, although he missed the flight, his equipment made the journey without him.

Thanks to a nasty ankle injury he picked up against Western Michigan, Felix wasn't fully fit. The chances of him playing that weekend? Slim to none. "I can still recall that moment when I got hurt, taking on Roger Lawson (running back)," he remembered. "Little did I know, *that play* might have saved my life."

Felix confesses that not a day goes by without memories of the crash seeping into his thoughts. Over the years, his dreams often transported him back, sometimes even having chats with his late teammates. He once shared with the *Cincinnati Enquirer,* during a heartfelt chat in December '06, the haunting memories from '70. The news of the crash reached him when he was chilling with buddies at the Student Union. Without wasting a second, he, along with a handful of Marshall athletes, jumped in a car and raced to the airport.

Once they arrived, they could only stand and watch, paralyzed by the biting cold and sheer horror. The crash left the mountainside smoldering in its aftermath. Jordan returned the next day, with the fires tamed, but the haunting smoke was still curling from the hill. He wished to aid in identifying his teammates, but the emotional weight was too much.

Felix grappled with the aftermath. Athletes, especially football players, are often pegged as epitomes of toughness, paragons of unyielding spirit. Tears? They're supposed to be alien to them. Yet, Felix couldn't care less about these "standards." All he could think of was the sudden void left by his teammates. They weren't just teammates; they were family. The abruptness of the loss was jarring, too intense to fathom. And yes, tears were shed.

Even now, Felix ponders the "why" behind his existence.

*****

Everyone was buzzing about Dickie Carter, nicknamed the "Sled Dog," thanks to his uncanny ability to drag tacklers after initial contact. At five feet, nine inches, and 225 pounds, this punishing fullback was on track to have a monster season. As a sophomore, Dickie dazzled as Marshall's top kickoff-return specialist. And when the Herd made a late-season turnaround in '69, Dickie was right at the forefront, averaging nearly 4.5 yards per carry. The stage was perfectly set for his senior year, with the Herd introducing the wishbone to their offense, spotlighting Dickie alongside Art Harris and Joe Hood. It was a trio made of dynamite! "Dickie should really help us this year," Coach Rick Tolley had predicted. And everyone believed it.

Life, however, is known to present unforeseen challenges. After a falling-out with Coach Tolley, Dickie felt he had no choice but to walk away, just two games into his final college season. Although many whispered of his absence, it was as if he vanished from Marshall's football history. The only glint of recognition? A fleeting one-second appearance in the documentary, *Ashes to Glory*. As Dickie puts it, "If you blink, you'll miss it." The pain of feeling forgotten, especially after his commitment to the team, weighed heavy on him. "I've heard that people felt like I betrayed the team," Dickie shared. "But if you'd seen me the night of the crash, my sense of loss was just as deep as anyone's. They were my teammates, my friends."

Even so, there's still one question that seems to linger on everyone's lips: Why did Dickie walk away? To get it, you have to understand the pressure cooker environment of Coach Tolley's practices. Nate Ruffin once described it like a boot camp in his recount of *The Marshall Story*. Tolley, endearingly referred to as the "Dog Man," was notorious for pushing players to their breaking point.

But after a crushing 52-3 loss to the University of Toledo, Dickie felt Coach Tolley pointed a finger at him, unfairly pinning the defeat largely on his shoulders. "After one of those grueling practices the week after the Toledo game, Tolley asked me if I owed him something (wind sprints)," Dickie recalled. "I took off my helmet, never used a curse word, and told him to shove it. And just like that, I walked off." Many of his teammates and even some assistant coaches whispered in his ear, urging him to return. Deep down, he hoped for a reconciliatory gesture from Coach Tolley. But that call never came. And with that, Dickie's time with the Thundering Herd ended, leaving behind a legacy of what might have been.

The plane crash occurred two days before Dickie's 22nd birthday (November 16). What should have been a Saturday evening of vibrant celebration for him turned tragically mournful. He was at a friend's off-campus apartment when the TV broadcast the shocking news: Marshall's plane had crashed. What followed was even more gut-wrenching—there were no survivors. Images of Marshall's backfield filled the screen, and there, unmistakably, was Dickie. In his hometown of Man, West Virginia, a tidal wave of shock gripped the residents. They believed they had just lost their beloved "Sled Dog."

The phone line at the Carter household was incessantly busy – ringing with concern, condolences, and confusion. Most folks in town had seen the newscast, and the distress was palpable. Yet, amidst the heartbreak, Dickie's mother stood resolute. "I just knew he was still alive," she'd later say, her voice unwavering. That deep maternal instinct, paired with her faith, assured her that if her son had perished, Almighty God would've whispered it to her.

Meanwhile, the grim scene at the crash site was an image Dickie could never have prepared for. Alongside Nate Ruffin, they could feel the blistering heat from the downed plane, even from their distant vantage point, roughly a quarter-of-a-mile away. The shadows of mourners, cast by the flames, danced in the night. Their whispered prayers and choked sobs created a heart-wrenching symphony. "It was like a dream," Dickie muttered. "My friends, my teammates—they were just... gone."

As the hours ticked by, Dickie felt trapped in a sorrowful haze. He tried repeatedly to reach his family, but the jammed phone lines offered no solace. Avoiding the melancholy that now enveloped the campus, Dickie sought refuge in his car. He drove around without purpose, the city's dim lights shimmering through the rain as tears blurred his vision. With dawn's first light, he finally connected with his family—a moment of piercing relief amidst the anguish. Yet, even in grief, the press was insatiable. They kept poking and prodding, trying to extract negative sentiments about Coach Tolley from him. The mere thought still brings a pang of sorrow to Dickie's heart. "The way they asked questions was cold and uncaring," he lamented. "I told them I didn't wish for him to be dead. Him being dead didn't change the fact that we didn't get along."

The aftermath of the tragedy upended Dickie's life. The once-vibrant campus now had an eerie aura. Echoes of laughter, camaraderie, spirited card games—all silenced. Lectures turned into tearful memorials as professors struggled with the roll calls. "I couldn't bear it," Dickie confided, his voice barely a whisper. "I wanted to go (to funerals), but it tore me up so badly, I just couldn't go. After a while, I decided against coming back to school. I couldn't go back. My mind wasn't right."

So, you see, for Dickie Carter, that chilling November night wasn't just a headline—it was an abrupt end to a chapter, forcing him onto a path of healing, away from the haunting memories of Marshall.

Even now, memories of the players' mood in the days prior to the crash are still crystal clear in Dickie's mind. Usually, the dorm echoed with laughter, the slap of playing cards, and the low hum of conversations. But in the days leading up to the crash, the atmosphere was unsettlingly different. The players sat scattered around, not in their usual boisterous clusters. Silence dominated, punctuated only by the occasional shuffle of feet or an uneasy sigh.

Dickie, leaning against a wall, scanned the scene. The weight of the atmosphere pressed down on him, forcing him to break the silence. He nudged Dave DeBord, the broad-shouldered offensive lineman lounging on a nearby couch. "Why all the sad faces?" Dickie inquired, trying to keep his voice light. Dave met Dickie's gaze, his usually sparkling eyes now shadowed with unease.

"Man, if I can just make it back from this trip, I'll count myself lucky."

Dickie, trying to infuse some optimism, countered, "Come on, Dave, it'll be fine."

But Dave merely shifted his gaze, his silence speaking volumes. The unsaid words hovered between them, like a cloud of apprehension. Across the room, tight end Freddy Wilson was engrossed in a quiet conversation. "I'd seriously take the truck with John Hagan rather than fly," he told a teammate. Dickie had heard about Hagan's superstition. The equipment manager had chosen to drive to East Carolina, citing a creepy narrative of a black bird crashing through his window on an ill-fated Friday the 13th. It was a tale that seemed to resonate with the team's palpable anxiety.

For years, the memory of that dormitory scene haunted Dickie. Night after night, he was jolted awake by nightmarish visions of the plane crash he had narrowly escaped. The dreams were always the same: flames, smoke, and him, standing amidst the wreckage. The visions were so disturbing that he had trouble going to sleep most of the time. So, he made a habit of sleeping with the lights on, and he started consuming a lot of alcohol as a means to cope. "That was the lowest point in my life," he confessed. "I was never suicidal, never became an alcoholic. But I've had thoughts that maybe I was supposed to be with them (on the plane). There are times when I feel like I let my teammates down because I wasn't there."

Seeking solace and understanding, Dickie frequently found himself at the doors of churches, confronting pastors with his anguish. "Would the Lord really take so many lives just to save a few?" he would plead, eyes desperate for answers. Each minister, with a mix of empathy and firmness, would reply, "Don't question God, Dickie. Every act of His has a purpose."

But for Dickie, those answers only intensified his search for clarity regarding the tragedy that left such a deep mark on his soul. The weight of those memories and emotions made the thought of going back to Marshall particularly daunting. Returning to MU was never an easy decision.

Back in '84, when a guest invitation to the Marshall Sports Hall of Fame banquet landed on his doorstep, there was a pause in the household. A pause that lingered like the hesitant quiet before a storm. Day after day, the weight of that invitation hung heavy on Dickie's mind. *"Should I go? What will they think of me?"* The fears of being rejected or shunned echoed in the quiet corridors of his memory. "I really didn't know if I would be accepted or not," Dickie admitted, with the raw honesty of a man who'd faced life's toughest battles.

If not for his wife and sister's gentle coaxing, the story might've been different. Yet, the two most important women in his life knew that this was a journey Dickie needed to take, not just for himself, but for the love of the game and the team he once called family. Walking into the induction dinner, the couple felt an overwhelming mix of nostalgia, hope, and trepidation. The room buzzed with the chatter of old teammates and friends, their laughter a comforting background sound. But then, slicing through the hum of conversation, came a voice that instantly sent waves of recognition through Dickie's soul:

"Sledddd!!!"

The call was like a blaring bull horn. Dickie didn't bother turning to see who was talking. He knew it was Reggie Oliver, the same man who had christened him with that unforgettable nickname, "Sled Dog." Reggie was being inducted into the Hall that night.

In that fleeting moment, as Reggie's voice wrapped around him, Dickie felt seen and remembered. Any fears or doubts were washed away by the power of those two words. The ambiance that had once felt spooky and eerie transformed into one of warmth and acceptance. "When Reggie yelled out 'Sled,' it made me feel a lot more at ease," Dickie reminisced, a soft smile lighting up his face.

Dickie's career on the field didn't end as he'd hoped, but it was filled with passionate plays, close-knit camaraderie, and memories that he'll treasure for a lifetime. "When I went back (to Marshall) all those years ago, things felt spooky and weird," he mused. "It was sad because I knew my teammates wouldn't be there. But now, things for me are much better than they were fifteen, twenty years ago." And while the pull of homecoming celebrations might not tug at his heartstrings as they do for others, Dickie has always been open about his journey and the lessons he's learned.

Several years ago, Dickie put pen to paper, sharing some of those reflections in a heartfelt letter to a schoolmate. And as his voice took on a more contemplative tone, he shared a snippet of those written words, words that encapsulated his spirit and philosophy:

"I've always been glad that I picked Marshall. I learned a lot of lessons ... but the hardest lesson I had to learn was how quick your life can change. I have had many events to cross my path since the crash, but there hasn't been anything that has affected my life that equals the magnitude of losing my teammates. Life has so many lessons to teach us. But I have found the most important one. It doesn't matter what team we may be on in life. When God calls our number the game is over."

And with that, Dickie's story reminds us of the fragile, fleeting nature of life, and the profound ways in which sports, camaraderie, and shared experiences shape our journeys.

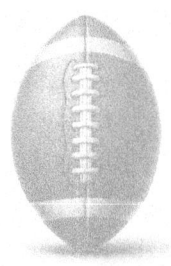

CHAPTER EIGHT

Turning the Page

Stepping onto the familiar streets of Jacksonville during Thanksgiving break in '70, I was hit with an unexpected chill. And it wasn't from the weather. Old friends looked at me as if they'd seen a ghost, their faces a mixture of relief and disbelief. "We thought you were gone," whispered a former high school football teammate, his voice trembling. Everywhere I went, the shadows of my past as a college athlete seemed to loom, intertwining with the recent tragedy that rocked Marshall University's football world. Most folks had pieced together a narrative from a Jacksonville newspaper article they'd read in the summer of '69, which painted a bright future for me in the Thundering Herd's secondary.

Fast forward to my junior year. Because of that story, the assumption was simple but horrifying: if I was still on the team, then surely I was on that doomed flight. And yet, here I was, no longer the "jock" from the article, but still very much entangled with the game I had played since fourth grade.

After the holidays, I returned to school, thinking I'd be covering student council meetings for *The Parthenon* (student newspaper). Instead, they handed me the hottest ticket in town: writing about the Marshall plane crash that dominated headlines and was dissected by every news outlet. I remember thinking, *"Is this real? Is my name really on the front page?"* Yep, there it was, my by-line on the story about the National Transportation Safety Board investigation diving deep into the crash.

But as fate would have it, life has a peculiar way of connecting our past, present and future. As I immersed myself in telling the story of the crash, fate reminded me of a time not so long ago, drawing me much closer to the heart of the tragedy than I could've ever anticipated.

A year earlier, I left the football field, hanging up my helmet for what I thought was the last time. In my mind, I was miles away from that plane, never imagining that under different circumstances, it could've been me on board that DC-9 jet that fateful night.

At the start of '71, whispers filled the halls about the state of MU football. *"Will they keep football going at Marshall?"* Some said it was the end. But deep down, I just *knew* the spirit of the game wouldn't fade. Besides, we had big names rooting for us, like Bill Cosby and Monte Hall (who raised money in a national telethon). And besides, not all our coaches were gone. Mickey Jackson, Carl Kokor, and Red Dawson were still around, but they were in limbo. "The big question was whether there would even be a next season," Mickey recalled. "We sat in the office day by day trying to determine if the school would keep the football program going."

In the days and weeks following the plane crash, Mickey Jackson recalls the overwhelming uncertainty he and the other Marshall assistant coaches faced regarding the future of Thundering Herd football. (Photo by Vic Simpson)

After the tragedy in November '70, rumors swirled about Marshall possibly dropping its football program. Quarterback Reggie Oliver, however, turned a deaf ear to these whispers. Choosing action over doubt, he spearheaded a monumental rebuild. (Photo courtesy of Marshall University)

Reggie Oliver, probably the next star QB, never flinched. "The varsity's gone, but we've still got our freshman team," he'd say with this glint in his eyes, making you believe football was immortal.

Then, in came Joe McMullen, the new athletics director. The buzz was that NFL legend Sam Huff was vying for the head coaching position. Heck, the man had charisma and credentials. But guess what? They didn't even give him an interview. Instead, we got Dick Bestwick, but just as quickly as he came, he left – two days later! Finally, they settled on Jack Lengyel from – wait for it – Wooster College. Ever heard of it? Me neither.

Feeling the weight of those memories of my former teammates, the guys who would never play again, I laced up my cleats and returned to the field. I remember that warm spring afternoon, the feeling of deja vu mixed with grief as I rushed down the Fairfield Stadium ramp for the first day of spring practice. But you know what? Every drop of sweat and every tackle brought a sliver of healing. Three weeks later, the world started to feel a bit more like it used to.

So, picture this: I'm standing in a sea of eager athletes, but this team? Man, they're like nothing I'd seen in my two years as a college player. Imagine a kaleidoscope of talent - most without any actual college football experience. Some from the freshman squad, others straight from the basketball court, and even a soccer player here and there. Some had memories of high school football, others? Well, they had nada. Zilch. Goose egg.

I remember this one time during practice, Rick Turnbow – an ex-basketball player now trying his hand as a tight end – made this rookie mistake. Guy's stretched out, going up for a catch, completely vulnerable. He's tall, lean, and every part of him screams "easy target." I could've totally taken him out. But then I realized, he hadn't yet learned to protect himself. So, I did the decent thing and backed off instead of going for the big hit. And you know what? That pass was badly overthrown.

As for the coaches? They were like chefs trying to make gourmet meals out of whatever was left in the fridge. They were dealing with raw material, and man, did they have to be creative! Coach Mickey

Jackson told me, "We didn't know how far we could push them. You had to be encouraging and supportive. We had to make adjustments in our coaching style. Every. Single. Day."

Then came the Varsity-Alumni game. Usually, it was a walk in the park for the varsity team, but this year, for '71? It could be a toss-up. The Alumni swaggered in, a whopping fifty of them, feeling good about their chances against this new, raw team. A larger than usual crowd of around 5,000 showed up to get a look at the practically brand-new Herd. But surprise, surprise! We shut them out, 26-0! Ed Carter later jokes, "They might've been good back in their day, but they were basically football retirees."

Fast forward a decade and guess who's playing for the Alumni? Yours truly! And, boy, did I feel it. My mind was racing, but my body? It felt like it was trudging through molasses!

Now, let's jump back in the time machine to that '71 game. The energy? Electric! Especially with Jim "Hillbilly" Preston, my ex-coach on the '68 freshman team, mouthing off throughout the game. Dude wouldn't shut up. And me? I lost it, busted my hand against his facemask and broke a few bones. Not my proudest moment.

These Varsity-Alumni games were like a high school reunion for the Alumni. They're there to party. Don't be shocked to see an old-timer chugging a cold one on the sidelines. Varsity players, on the other hand, are there to prove themselves. The spring is the time for many to move up the depth chart for the fall season when the games really count.

Oh, and let's not forget the jersey fiasco on the day of the game! I get to the stadium, and guess which jersey I'm handed? No. 40 – the number that Larry "Dupree" Sanders' used to wear. The memories with Dupree in that jersey flooded back. I hesitated, but didn't want to kick up a fuss. So, I wore it. But nothing prepared me for that final moment that night. As the game wound down, with the defense trotting off the field, I spotted Macie Lugo, Dupree's girlfriend, in the crowd. The pain, the nostalgia, it was all there in her eyes. She called out, "Hey! Craig Teeee, number for-teeee!" Throat got tight. I was lost for words. All I could do was wave, with a smile, and a heart full of memories.

The exhilaration and camaraderie of the Varsity-Alumni game had brought a temporary sense of unity and celebration to the Marshall community. Yet, beneath the surface of cheerful springtime activities, there lingered a shadow from the previous year's events. The memories of the November 13th fights still weighed heavily on the collective conscience of the school, particularly within the black-student community.

During the months following the crash, there was deep concern that administrators would do everything in their power to punish all blacks who participated in the Friday the 13th melee. Within the black-student community, some feared that a wholesale expulsion was in the works. During the spring of '71, ten black students were charged with assault and battery in cases filed in the school's student court.

In the hallowed halls and bustling classrooms, a thick tension seemed to hang in the air. There was this collective gut feeling that the blacks facing charges would soon find themselves pushed out, almost like old leaves swept off by a brisk wind. You see, when you glanced at the student court, it was hard to ignore the blatant imbalance. Out of the five arbiters of justice, which consisted of four students and a single MU faculty member, only one face mirrored their own – and that was Bill Redd. Yet, against the grim anticipation and the odds that seemed to lean heavily in one direction, not a single expulsion occurred. It was like the sun breaking through a week-long stormy forecast.

Bill, the lone black judge, leaned in, voice tinged with a mix of passion and relief about the proceedings. "The motive behind those charges? Crystal clear. They wanted to boot them out. Each and every one of them." He paused, perhaps reliving that moment. "But the narrative they were peddling didn't hold water. They painted a picture where all the blame was squarely put on the black students." He shook his head, eyes narrowing, "But I was there. I witnessed the initial spark that set everything off."

Bill's voice, filled with emotion, described the chaotic scene. Right after the game, he recalls seeing a young man gleefully sprinting down the field, the Rebel flag flapping wildly behind him. "By doing that, it was like throwing a lit match near a jug of kerosene. Fights broke out. Fists flying, lots of shouting. I had to pry one guy off another. It was a nightmarish moment."

With Bill Redd's words, you could almost feel the weight of that day, the sharp sting of injustice, and the chaos that had unraveled. But above all, the narrative highlighted a triumphant stand against prejudice, even within the confines of a seemingly lopsided system. As the dust settled from the acquittal of the black students who were charged with assault and battery, the MU atmosphere began to hum with a different energy. The resilience of those students became a beacon of hope and strength for many. The latter part of August signaled the onset of a new academic year and a fresh start. The '71 fall football season was about to commence for the Thundering Herd, and with it came the anticipation of new challenges and new beginnings.

The dawn of fall practice in '71 marked a truly special moment. You see, the NCAA had handed Marshall a shimmering golden ticket – a special exemption which allowed freshmen to play varsity football. Imagine that! The palpable buzz of excitement was practically electric, radiating from every corner of the field. Freshmen and sophomores, a tidal wave of youthful vigor, flooded the roster, and thus, the "Young Thundering Herd" was born.

However, my personal journey on the gridiron took an unexpected turn. After just three intense weeks of preseason practice, I found myself demoted to back-up duty. A new competitor stepped onto the field: a transfer named Gene Nance, who bore a legacy of football excellence like a cherished family heirloom. His elder brother, Jim Nance, starred at Syracuse University and played seven seasons in the American Football League, mostly with the Boston Patriots as league MVP and a three-time All-Star pick.

I stepped away from the game, not a trace of remorse clinging to my departure. Football's rhythm was no longer my heartbeat. My passion to play was gone for good. Yet, an invisible thread still wove me into its fabric. Fate, with an uncanny sense of irony, planted me in an apartment *across the street* from where the Young Thundering Herd played. Talk about serendipity dripping from every eave! From my lofty perch on the third floor, I gazed upon the unfolding spectacle – a patchwork view partially obstructed by the scoreboard's watchful eye. Still, I was perched in a bird's nest of sports, the announcer's voice painting the action as vividly as if I sat among the roaring crowd. A front-row ticket gifted by proximity.

Regrets? Nah, not a one. The echo of cleats hitting turf, the adrenaline-spiked crescendos of cheers – they didn't haunt my dreams. The athlete within me had penned its final chapter, but my story danced on, pirouetting towards journalism. I envisioned newsprint and ink-stained fingers, a destiny etched in words and stories. Little did I fathom that the sports arena would beckon me once more, not as a player, but as a storyteller. As a journalist and a photographer – I roamed the varied landscapes of athletics, from the grand stages to the local fields, capturing the essence of competition through the lens of my craft.

Although I said sayonara to football, I still had an intense interest in the game. As things turned out, I got the thrill of a lifetime as an eyewitness to the Herd's heart-stopping win over Xavier University (Ohio). It was the first home game of the '71 season. The echoes of that victory still reverberate throughout the annals of college football history. It wasn't just a game; it was a clash of underdogs and giants that produced a boatload of intrigue, suspense, and jubilation..

Picture it: Fairfield Stadium, packed to the brim like a treasure chest stuffed with hopes and dreams. A record-setting crowd of 13,000 strong had gathered, drawn by the allure of the Young Thundering Herd. Xavier was supposed to be the Goliath for that day. But oh, how appearances can be deceiving. In the weeks leading up to this contest, murmurs of skepticism hung in the air. Even so, Marshall, the clear underdog, held its own. As the first quarter played out, Blake Smith, a soccer player who transformed himself into a placekicker, booted a thirty-one-yard field goal. The scoreboard read 3-0, Marshall's favor. Now, there was a gust of optimism in the storm of doubt.

As the battle raged on, Xavier flexed its muscles and seized a 13-9 lead in the fourth quarter. The Herd, however, wasn't about to surrender. The game clock kept ticking, the minutes slipping away. But the hearts of Marshall's faithful beat louder with each passing second. They could feel it in their bones – a comeback was brewing. Then, like a bolt of lightning, it happened. One minute and eighteen seconds left on the clock. Marshall's last stand. A defensive blitz forced a three-and-out. After a punt, the ball found its resting place near midfield, and with a warrior's resolve, the Thundering Herd charged forth.

A couple of fourth-down conversions ensued, each one a breath of possibility. Now, the clock was friend and foe, ticking down the seconds with every snap. There was still a chance, a glimmer of the improbable. Hope hung in the air like a kite.

Amidst the chaos, there I sat, perched in the corner bleachers of the south end zone, watching history in the making. Lanny Steed, the freshman sensation, was unstoppable, a comet streaking across the field (8 catches for 113 yards). The ball rested on Xavier's thirteen-yard line, and Reggie Oliver, the maestro of this symphony, stood poised.

Nine seconds.

Eight seconds.

Seven seconds.

The stadium held its collective breath as Reggie led the charge. The tension was unbelievable and Marshall's sideline was a whirlwind of emotion, a tempest of urgency. "Get the play off, Reggie! Get the play off, Reggie!" a chorus of voices yelled from the MU bench.

Three seconds.

Two seconds...

"Hut, hut!"

The snap, the heartbeats of an entire stadium synchronized with the rhythm of the game. The Marshall QB's eyes scanned the field like a hawk, and then, in a heartbeat, it was over. The final gun sounded .....

Reggie 's sleight of hand was a masterpiece. A play-fake, a roll to the right, a glance to the corner, and then a pivot to the unexpected. Terry Gardner emerged from the shadows, catching the ball like a dream. The defense, fooled by misdirection, crumbled. And there, like a guardian of destiny, was Jack Crabtree, the behemoth offensive tackle, clearing the path. Gardner made a mad dash to the end zone.

Touchdown Herd!!!

Marshall 15, Xavier 13.

The stadium erupted in a sonic boom of jubilation that shattered doubt and left a lasting imprint on history. A wave of fans surged onto the field, their overwhelming joy could not be contained. And so, in its home opener of '71, the Thundering Herd defied the odds, etching its name into the tapestry of college football greatness. ESPN's Top 100 plays of all time proudly showcases Marshall's game-winning play as its No. 83 – a testament to the power of perseverance and the beauty of the underdog spirit.

No one who stood in Fairfield Stadium that day could ever erase the memory from their minds. The ground seemed to tremble with emotion, the air electrified with exhilaration. Even hours after the final whistle, a sea of people lingered, soaking in the glory of the moment. Tears streamed down some faces, while others screamed with unbridled joy, as if they'd just struck the jackpot in a sweepstakes. Coach Mickey Jackson emerged from the locker room, fresh from a shower, dressed in his post-game attire. The sight before him was astonishing. "The celebration seemed like it lasted the rest of the evening," he reminisced. "Stepping back out, the stands looked like we were still in the heart of the fourth quarter."

This was no ordinary win. It was an uplifting triumph, yes, but it also stood as a poignant tribute to those lost in the tragic plane crash the year before. Yet, that season had another victory too: a narrow 12-10 win over Bowling Green for Homecoming.

Amidst staggering challenges, the '71 Marshall team held the line, preventing the potential collapse of the program. In some ways, I wish I had been there with them. But, life had other plans for me. Earnestine and I had just tied the knot, and our son, Carlos Greenlee, was soon to grace our lives, arriving a mere four days before my 21st birthday. Yet, family life didn't lead me away from the team. When I walked away from the '71 season, it was a personal choice, unrelated to injuries or scandals. Simply, it was my time to step aside.

Surprisingly, years later, I received an invitation to a reunion for that very team. I politely declined, writing back to express my reasons. I had chosen to part ways before the season truly began, so I felt it wouldn't be right to claim my place among them. But, the stories of that time and those games live vividly in my memory.

The plane crash, the subsequent challenging seasons; they could've grounded the Herd. Yet, the enduring power of resilience was clear for all to see. It would be over a decade after the '71 Xavier game before Thundering Herd followers witnessed the glorious rise of a revived program.

And oh, what a rise it was! From the triumphant 6-5 finish in 1984, marking the first winning season in twenty years, to the heartaches in the late '80s and early '90s, every step of the journey was marked by unwavering grit. Then, in 1992, a moment of sheer magic: Willy Merrick's last-second field goal gave Marshall its first national championship. The highs and lows continued, with the legendary Randy Moss setting records in 1996, and the breathtaking comeback led by quarterback Byron Leftwich in the GMAC Bowl of 2001.

Coach Mickey Jackson firmly believes that '71 was the game-changer for Marshall. "Had we not persisted, waiting even a decade or two to resurrect football, it would've been starting from scratch," he mused. ""There would've been no momentum whatsoever. Because the school kept the program going, it continued to build and build."

CHAPTER 9

Following Father

Delongelo Brown, a Marshall graduate and former football player, finds solace and inspiration whenever he returns to the school where his father, Larry "the Governor" Brown once played. (Photo by Vic Simpson)

From the moment Delongelo Brown slipped into that football uniform, one gifted to him as a 4-year old, he *knew*. "The game came naturally to me. Always felt I was destined to be a football player," he explains. With every step in those pads, grandmother Mary Byrd Walker's voice echoed on Christmas morning: "Well look at you, walking around here like you know exactly what to do on a football field." This wasn't just a uniform; it was destiny.

But behind destiny's calling, there's a shadow of a memory. The life of Delongelo's father, Larry "the Governor" Brown, came to a tragic end when Marshall's plane went down. Delongelo was almost three at that time. Though a toddler's memories fade, the legend of "the Governor" or simply "Gov" never did. To many, he was a legend. To Delongelo, he was the father he never got to know. "It was hurtful for me to go to sports awards banquets and see other kids with their fathers there to support them," he shares, raw emotion dripping from every word. Time hasn't entirely healed the wound; at 56, with grown children of his own, the void is still palpable.

Delongelo's son carries a special name – it's Governor Larry Brown. He's making waves as a software engineer and building his own legacy. As for daughter Jolisa, she's another testament to the family's enduring spirit. Aside from being a talented software engineer, she speaks fluent Spanish and French, and has a degree from Rice University. On a related note, the Brown patriarch shared this snippet. "My son was curious about his first name," he said with a smile, "I just told him that I gave him his granddad's cherished football nickname." Pretty neat, huh?

Growing up, Delongelo always felt an empty space where those treasured dad-kid memories should've been. He deeply recognizes the irreplaceable magic of fatherly bonds. Now, as a father himself, it's not just a role for him but a pure, unfiltered joy. "I never had those father/child moments growing up, so you savor those moments when they come," he reflected, his voice tinged with a mix of nostalgia and pride. "I truly believe that our kids mirror what we pour into them. So, you bet I'm giving my all to give them the best."

Memories and recollections of his deceased father were always agonizing for Brown as a youngster. Like an old photograph, his mother, Shirley Walker, painted vivid pictures of "the Governor." Yet, these tales were often punctuated with tears, "The subject of my Dad has always produced a lot of pain," he recalls. "Mom would tell me about him and start crying as if it happened yesterday." Yet, amidst the tears, the essence of a father emerged.

There was this one memory, where the Governor, clad in somber black, hinted about a premonition to Shirley. His words were piercing: "I have a life insurance policy, so if something happens to me, I want you to promise me... you take the money and get a house, so my son won't have to grow up in the ghetto." At that time, home was "The Bluff," an Atlanta district notorious for high crime rates and high drug traffic, most notably heroin. Definitely not a place to raise a family. Shirley Walker honored that request, providing shelter not just for her son, but for a mini-squadron of extended family members. "What my Dad did shows that he was wise beyond his years," Delongelo asserts with pride. Thanks to the Governor, generations shifted from despair to opportunity, from danger to safety.

However, life took a turn when Delongelo lost that cherished house in a divorce. But the fire in him burns undeterred. He's set his eyes on reclaiming that abode, which isn't just brick and mortar but a bridge to his past. "That home has so many memories for me," he says, a soft gleam in his eyes. "It's the one thing that helps me feel connected to my Dad."

The seeds for young Brown's football stardom were sown during pre-season practice in his freshman year at Therrell High School. When the chance to play linebacker on the school's B team beckoned, he was ordered to leave the field. Why? No mouthpiece. Fate, however, had a trick up its sleeve! In the dirt, there it was: a discarded mouthpiece. "Everybody saw me pick it up, and they yelled out... e-uuuuuuu, you so nasty!" Delongelo defiantly ignored all comments. He could care less. With each play, he showcased his skill set, evolving into the defensive dynamo everyone would soon know and fear.

But to give you a clearer picture of the road Delongelo had traveled, let's rewind. Imagine a six-year old boy surrounded by the watchful eyes of five uncles and a few hard-nosed football coaches. It's like a scene from a movie – the young, rebellious spirit, refusing to bend or bow. But when a coach's boot met Delongelo's behind during a football drill, he took his stand and headed home. Can you picture Grandma's surprise, seeing him back so soon? "I quit the team," he declared. This didn't sit right with grandma, so she summoned the uncles. Their mission? Teach this young'un the real meaning of resilience.

Yes, Delongelo learned a lesson about staying the course and not giving up. But in spite of all this collective guidance he was getting, his inclination for mischief continued to show. And it happened when he was 7.

Against Grandma's stern warning, Delongelo hooked up with some older boys, ages 11 and 12. Days were filled with playing ball, riding bikes, and fishing in the nearby woods, where a seemingly abandoned house stood. Curiosity gripped the boys, and being the smallest, young Brown was hoisted to crawl through a cracked window. What followed was a reckless act of childhood: they ransacked the house. This mischief led to police intervention, but thanks to the incredulity of the neighbors ("You're arresting babies now?") and a finger-pointing friend known for spinning tall tales, the kids, Delongelo among them in handcuffs, were soon released. The message was clear: watch the company you keep.

However, lessons from childhood often need reinforcement. High school saw Brown, the teenager, hooking up with another rowdy group, "The Dog Crew." Composed mainly of fellow football players, their weekends were often marred by brawls, leading to their infamous ban from the Six Flags Over Georgia theme park. "Always on the verge of getting locked up," he said. Delongelo's lucky streak lasted until one fateful evening, walking home from football practice, he ordered some snacks and a drink from a food truck, and walked away without paying. It was only a matter of time before the law caught up. When he got home, the police were sitting on his doorstep. The next stop – juvenile court.

The courtroom was a grim setting. Yet, in an unexpected turn, the judge, a football enthusiast, recognized Brown's name - not from any criminal record but from the All-City football team roster. With full restitution made by Joseph Cain, his supportive stepfather, Delongelo was granted a second chance, coupled with a stern warning.

Football might have catapulted Delongelo into the limelight, but it wasn't all touchdowns and roaring crowds. There were dark alleys and tempting turns. Yet, amid the chaos, two shining lights emerged in his life, fighting fiercely to keep him grounded: his radiant girlfriend, Alysia Stinchcomb, and his industrious stepdad.

Delongelo wasn't just rocking the football field; he was also scrubbing floors, wiping windows and vacuuming carpets. That's right! Thanks to Joseph's cleaning business, he found himself elbow-deep in soapy water instead of street troubles. And it wasn't just about the money. It was Joseph's sly way of ensuring that his stepson spent less time calling shots on the streets and more time hustling legitimately. Meanwhile, Alysia wasn't just a girlfriend. She was a source of encouragement, lighting up Brown's life, and inadvertently, cutting his 'crew-time' down drastically.

"Without Alysia and my stepdad," Delongelo admits with a heartfelt sigh, "things probably would've turned out a lot worse." No doubt, their presence in his life proved to be a game-changer. They offered him not just love and work, but new directions to unleash his boundless energy.

By the time his senior year was winding down, Delongelo wasn't your average defensive player. He was a beast as a rover linebacker, making waves and grabbing All-City team accolades. And the cherry on top? Bagging the Golden Helmet Award - a shining badge of honor, marking him as the MVP of Therrell's football program. College scouts were drooling, but there was a hiccup. His height. Though he was officially listed as 5-foot-9, whispers had it he was closer to 5-foot-6. And while some might've seen this as a setback. Not this guy. He assumed the role of master magician by creating an illusion of being taller on videotape than in real life.

When it came time to pick a college, Delongelo was pretty set on Liberty University. But things took a turn when he sat through a sermon by Rev. Jerry Falwell, the school's co-founder. "It was so political," he'd say with a shrug. "For me, that was a big turn-off. My church always talked about Jesus."

Enter Tim Mitchell, a hotshot linebacker from nearby Decatur. He wouldn't stop chirping in Delongelo's ear about the awesomeness of Marshall and how the school was recruiting some serious talent from Georgia. And if that wasn't tempting enough, MU dangled a quick-expiring plane ticket for him to check out its turf. Yet, there was a plot twist. Marshall was close to Brown's heart because of his Dad's legacy. Although memories of the plane crash made his Mom apprehensive, the nostalgia and connection could not be easily dismissed.

The move to the college level mandated that the Governor's son would have to switch positions. Tight ends in college are typically much bigger than they are in high school. So, instead of being a rover linebacker, he switched over to cornerback. Delongelo bided his time as a back-up and waited eagerly to parlay his skills in the '88 Spring Game. This was his golden ticket to prove himself and earn a football scholarship. All game long, he was matched up against All-American wide receiver Mike Barber, who would go on to play four seasons in the NFL. The end result? A monstrous performance from Brown, limiting the standout receiver in ways that left everyone stunned.

After the game, Fairfield Stadium was alive with an electrifying energy. While most spring games were simple affairs, this was something special. It was a celebration of a journey marked by blood, sweat and sheer grit. Just five months earlier, each player had been part of the Thundering Herd's journey to the NCAA Division 1-AA national championship game. As their names echoed throughout the stadium, a crowd of 7,000 erupted in cheers. "I remember thinking, wow, all these people are clapping for me," Delongelo reminisced. "I stood there just soaking it in."

Long before his breakout spring game, however, Delongelo received some crucial advice from Jerome Hazard, a fellow football player who had noticed a concerning academic issue. Delongelo had amassed plenty of elective hours, but he fell woefully short in taking the required courses for his major. This realization served as a wake-up call. Up until then, he had simply followed his academic advisors' recommendations regarding his class selection. "Jerome made me realize that I was a solid year behind (in core courses for my major)," Delongelo said. "So, I became even more dedicated to my studies."

Reflecting on the spring game, Delongelo was ecstatic about his exceptional performance. However, over the course of the summer of '88, a deafening silence set in. Despite giving his all and even receiving a ring commemorating the team's achievements, a scholarship offer remained elusive. It was this, combined with Jerome Hazard's earlier advice, that led to a critical decision. As pre-season practice began, Delongelo was conspicuously absent. "Obtaining that college degree became my dream, my true purpose," he declared, determination evident in his voice. "Having those conversations with Jerome felt like a divine intervention."

Navigating college with limited resources was like scaling a steep, unforgiving mountain. Yet, Delongelo braved these odds with an unwavering spirit. The hard-earned dollars from his Atlanta warehouse gig and working on summertime construction crews became his tuition lifeline, and his position in Marshall's Admissions Office added a financial buffer. Beyond finances, the camaraderie of his Kappa Alpha Psi brothers and the steadfast support of his girlfriend, Lynn Moore, became his emotional anchors, ensuring he was never adrift or hungry. Delongelo continued to streamline his priorities and bravely took on a daunting 21-hour course load in his final semester of college. Through all the adversities and challenges, Delongelo earned his Bachelor's degree in business.Talk about a power play!

While Delongelo's incredible journey to earn his college degree showcased his gritty perseverance, it's only one part of his remarkable story. His path took a poignant turn when an old news article and photograph of his father, initially evoking profound grief, gradually transformed into a powerful source of inspiration. This article, sent to him by his paternal grandmother, Bessie Bethea, captured a historical moment: Marshall's "Governor" standing beside West Virginia's Governor, Arch Moore, during Marshall's season opener vs. Morehead State in '70 (Herd won 17-7).

That day, as the tale goes, "Gov" Brown jokingly told Governor Moore that a photo with him would seal his re-election. As history would have it, Moore did indeed secure back-to-back terms ('68 through '76), and even a third term in '84. To Delongelo, this photo bore deep significance. In his sixth-grade Career Day, he proudly presented it to share his father's story. However, his teacher's skepticism made him feel small and invalidated.

Years later, a serendipitous encounter led Delongelo's wife, Alysia, to this very teacher. Holding onto her outdated perception, the teacher was taken aback to learn of Delongelo's accomplishments. This revelation changed how Delongelo viewed the old photograph. It wasn't just about refuting a past slight, but celebrating the legacies of both him and his father.

Looking back, Delongelo reflects, "That picture used to remind me of that embarrassing day in sixth grade. But now, it gives me a huge sense of triumph. When I ran into my old teacher, I proudly showed her my ring (from Marshall playing in a national championship game) and spoke about my career with a Fortune 500 company. I took satisfaction in her coming to understand how wrong she was about how my life would turn out. The whole time we talked, she had this confused look on her face. No doubt, success is the sweetest revenge."

Just as his past intertwined with his present in unexpected ways, Delongelo would discover that the echoes of yesteryears can reemerge in the most unforeseen circumstances.

Several years after college graduation, Delongelo discovered just how vivid memories of his father were among those who'd known him. The discovery came in 2008, from an unlikely source—his former college roommate at Marshall, Edgar Froe. While getting a haircut in Atlanta, Edgar engaged in a discussion about college football with a barber, an ardent Florida fan. Edgar mentioned that during the decade of the '90s, Marshall's Thundering Herd was the winningest football program in NCAA Division I.

An elderly man waiting his turn for a barber chimed in, "Did you say Marshall? I knew a man who died in that plane crash. His name was Larry Brown."

A wave of realization hit Edgar. "Larry Brown? I roomed with his son at Marshall!"

The old man's eyes softened, "I've kept a certificate that belonged to Larry in my car for ages, hoping to one day give it to his son."

They coordinated a meeting with Delongelo. There, with evident emotion, the elderly man handed over a letterman's certificate from Larry's high school years. It celebrated Larry's achievements in football and track. For Delongelo, this unexpected find was overwhelming. "It's like getting a piece of my dad back," he whispered.

Memories of his father continue to loom large for Delongelo. He's often drawn into an emotional whirlwind whenever his father is mentioned. The pain, still sharp and deep-rooted, is one reason he's never been able to watch the *We Are Marshall* movie in its entirety.

In 2023, another unexpected event underscored the rawness of his emotions. While finalizing a sale at a Toyota dealership, Delongelo experienced an unexpected resurgence of his deep sorrow when a customer commented about the Marshall memorabilia in his workspace. Overwhelmed, he excused himself momentarily. Later, he cleared all such items from his area. "It still cuts deep," Delongelo admits. "Sometimes, I avoid talking about it. But knowing Marshall remembers my dad reassures me he didn't live in vain."

Delongelo's life, filled with challenges and unexpected turns, speaks to his resilience. Keep in mind that during his football-playing days, he was a walk-on and was never awarded a scholarship. His journey isn't just about survival but triumph. It's a testament to his determination and spirit. In the face of adversity, Delongelo Brown stands as proof that with heart and perseverance, one can overcome any obstacle.

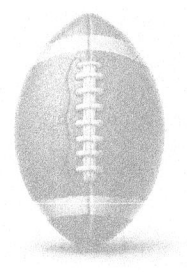

CHAPTER 10

A Family's Voyage Through Grief

In the heart of Virginia, where football threads through the very fabric of its communities, Frank Loria emerged as more than just an athlete. Virginia Tech's stadium pulsed with energy, and at its core was Frank, a two-time All-American who made the game look like an art form. But when the roar of the crowd faded and the stadium lights dimmed, Frank wore another hat—that of a devoted husband to Phyllis and a doting father to Victoria and Julie. And as the Loria family awaited their newest member, Frank Jr., the horizon glowed with hope and dreams of shared tomorrows.

Then, in an instant that no one saw coming, tragedy struck. The plane bearing the Marshall University football team, with Frank onboard as an assistant coach, went down, and there were no survivors. As the news reverberated, hearts across the country, especially in Virginia, shattered. Amidst the loss, Phyllis, eight months pregnant, faced the daunting task of navigating a world without her partner. She had to keep their children's memories of their father alive, while bracing herself for the birth of a son who would never meet his dad. All the children are now in their 50's, each carrying forward a piece of Frank's legacy, with the stories, values and memories passed down to them.

This chapter delves into the resilience of a family faced with the unthinkable, the legacy of a young legend, and the community that nurtured them with compassion and cherished memories. It's a testament to the spirit of Frank Loria, whose memory remains as indelible as the footprints he left on the football field.

Portrait of Love and Resilience

In her younger years, Phyllis Loria-Riccelli (known then as Phyllis Loria) was blindsided by a tragedy that plunged her into a whirlwind of pain and disbelief. At 23, she had been the vibrant heart of her family, with two beautiful toddler daughters and another bundle of joy on the horizon. But then came the fateful night of the plane crash, casting an indelible mark on her soul. The radio's grim announcement hung in the air, heavy with dread. Surrounded by her family, a cocoon of warmth and concern, they exchanged glances that spoke a thousand words - fear, disbelief, and a faint hope that there might be survivors.

A collective decision was made, one rooted in love and concern for her well-being. They shielded Phyllis from the full magnitude of the tragedy, guiding her through the darkness. Her mother-in-law's wise advice, spoken softly, like a shield against harm, reminded her of the little ones relying on her resilience. "Phyllis, let's get through this," said Erma Loria in a calm, reassuring tone of voice. "Remember, you carry life within and you have two little girls to take care of."

Sensing the unbearable tension building up after a couple of nerve-wracking days, Phyllis's parents took charge. They packed a few bags and whisked Phyllis and the kids away to Clarksburg, West Virginia, desperate to shield her from the intensifying emotional storm in Huntington as she anxiously awaited that heart-wrenching call. A full week passed by before Frank Loria was identified.

Just before the calendar flipped to welcome the New Year, baby Frank Loria Jr. made his entrance into the world, bringing with him joy laced with sorrow. This tiny bundle was the silver lining of Phyliss's storm, but she was heartbroken knowing he would never feel his father's embrace. "It was so rewarding, but at the same time, so tragic," Phyllis remembers. "And that's because Frank wouldn't be there to help raise him. I was able to work my way through things because of my faith.

That's why I didn't fall apart. But I really had no choice. I had to be super strong for everybody involved."

The true test of Phyllis's resilience came when she returned to Marshall in '71. The occasion? The Herd's home opener against Xavier University (Ohio). It was the first regular season game at Fairfield Stadium since the plane crash 10 months earlier. Walking back into that charged atmosphere felt like reopening a fresh wound. Phyllis recalled, "It was as if death hit me in the face. I was in a fog. But the young players deserved for us to be there." Even so, every moment was a stark reminder of Frank. But when she saw the faces of the children whose parents died in the crash, that was the final blow. "They were orphans and it was so sad," she said in a somber tone that echoed her deep hurt. "It felt like I was at the funeral all over again. So, I told myself, I cannot put myself in that place again." It would be ages before Phyllis could bring herself to return to Marshall.

As seasons changed and years passed, one tradition remained unchanged in Phyllis's household. Every year, like clockwork, they remembered Frank's birthday with a fervent celebration. A day marked with both joy and reflection, it wasn't merely a remembrance. It was a symphony of love, a dedication to a legacy that wouldn't be forgotten. With unwavering determination, Phyllis constructed an intricate mosaic of memories, drawing on stories from those who were closest to him. Family, friends, and former teammates - they all played a vital role in keeping his spirit alive in the hearts of the children.

At every possible opportunity, the family spent time with Frank Beamer, the renowned Hokies coach who was one of Frank's college teammates. As Beamer recounted tales of Loria's skills and personality, the past came alive, every word echoing with emotion and reverence. And then, in the scenic heart of Blacksburg, Virginia, the Loria siblings experienced a moment of profound significance. They were there, right at the epicenter, when Virginia Tech retired their father's iconic #10 jersey, ensuring that his legacy would forever be etched in the school's history.

Jerry Claiborne, who coached Loria at Virginia Tech, was another stalwart presence. His insights offered a glimpse into the depth of

Loria's talent and passion. When the monumental day came for Loria to be inducted into the College Football Hall of Fame, the atmosphere was thick with pride and nostalgia. Claiborne stood there, alongside the children, witnessing a well-deserved tribute to a phenomenal player and person.

This family's journey was an ever-evolving tapestry of moments, from grand ceremonies to intimate family gatherings. Emotions always ran high, with tears often flowing freely. Yet, those tears were interwoven with laughter, joy, and a deep sense of belonging. Surrounded by tales of valor, love, and determination, the children grew up with an intimate knowledge of a father they never knew, but whom they profoundly revere.

In a world filled with fleeting moments, Phyllis carved out a timeless haven. She cultivated a home sanctuary where family was always welcome to visit and stay over. Through her resilience, she shielded her children from the overbearing weight of grief. But she also wore her heart on her sleeve when November 14th rolled around. It was a day drenched in melancholy, where tears would inevitably fall. "It was tough," she reminisces. "Every year on November 14th, the kids would see me cry."

Life, however, has a way of surprising us with unexpected blessings. And in '74, Phyllis married Clifton Garner, a man who stepped in not as a replacement, but as a pillar. Their bond spanned 13 years, with Clifton recognizing the infinite space the children held in Phyllis's heart and respecting it. Instead of the cold title of "stepfather," he was lovingly embraced as the Loria siblings "second dad."

By the time 1999 rolled around, love came knocking again. Richard Riccelli, with his warm heart and impeccable culinary skills, entered their lives. The grandchildren lovingly dubbed him "Poppi." Laughter and the aroma of Italian cooking wafted through their home, with debates over who made the best dishes. "Rich's Italian dishes are sometimes better than mine. So says my kids," Phyllis chuckles. "But I don't get upset about it. He loves cooking for them and that makes me happy."

For Phyllis, life was more than just shades of sorrow. It bore patches of radiant joy, like in 2000, when she stood before the "We Are Marshall" wall sculpture at Edwards Stadium. For the first time, tears of grief didn't blur her vision.

Six years later, an exclusive, by-invitation-only screening of the film *We Are Marshall* in Huntington, became another cherished moment. It was an intimate event where families, forever changed by the crash, gathered. With bated breath and teary eyes, she witnessed a cinematic tribute that perfectly captured the spirit of the '70 team. "It was very touching," she said. "I was so proud to be a part of that. The movie remembered them in such a beautiful way."

Victoria's journey

Ever hear the story of Victoria Buchner, the eldest Loria kid? She was just about 3 when her dad tragically passed away. Imagine, just three, and yet she's got this one vibrant memory of him. She was visiting her grandparents in Clarksburg, minding her toddler business, when a dog started chasing her. But just as her tiny heart raced, her superhero - her dad - swooped in, saving the day. "I was awfully young, but I do remember that," she reminisces. "Dad saved me from getting chewed up. He was there to protect me. That was a tender moment."

And you know what's heartbreaking? That might be her only real-time memory, but she's got this old photo - it's of Frank sprawled on the floor, worn out from his long days as an assistant college football coach at Marshall. And there she is, a toddler, poking him, as if to say, "Come on, Dad, let's play, let's hang out." Just looking at that picture, you can sense the bond they would've shared. Over the years, Victoria stumbled upon his letters - heart-warming stuff written to his wife and his mother. "Think about that for a moment," she said. "With everything that was going on in his life, he found the time to write letters to the people who were important to him. All those letters are centered on family."

Fast forward to 2006. As the buzz around the movie *We Are Marshall* grew, Victoria found herself in a poignant conversation, admitting she had never heard her dad's voice. That's when fate, or perhaps a kind twist of coincidence, intervened. Rosalyn Queen, a close friend of the family, did some digging and handed Victoria a 39-year-old black & white videotape of the '67 All-America football team on the Bob Hope

Show. Big football names were all there, including O.J. Simpson. On that tape, the players came out one by one, identifying themselves and naming their respective schools.

Trotting out to center stage with a bounce in his gait, Frank Loria confidently introduced himself: "Frank Loria, Virginia Tech." Quick to jest, Bob Hope shot back, "Frank's really a speedster. You'd be fast too if you got your training running out of sorority houses!" While the audience's laughter filled the air, it was Frank's bashful smirk that lingered in Victoria's memory. Watching that tape, she reflected, "That was really cool. For me, it was more than hearing the sound of his voice. Seemed like he might be a little on the shy side. But it was good to see some of his personality. You can't get a feel for that just by looking at pictures."

As much as Victoria treasures all memories of her father, she always avoided attending the annual Marshall memorial fountain ceremony. I mean, who could blame her? Revisiting the pain and anguish each year? But life's funny, and a chance encounter with Parker Ward Jr., an avid Marshall supporter whose father was also on that ill-fated plane, changed everything. Ward came to town when Marshall played at Virginia Tech. Being told of Victoria's resistance, he made an intriguing offer. *"Take this ring for now, but you have to promise me that you'll give it back. To do that, you have to come to the ceremony in Huntington."* This wasn't some random ring – it was a championship ring representing Marshall's victory in the '92 NCAA Division I-AA national title game.

Initially, she dreaded making the trip. But it wasn't long before her outlook changed dramatically. Victoria found solace, tears mixed with smiles, in that gathering. "I thought it would be too much to handle emotionally," she remembers. "It brings back horrible memories and thoughts about what could have been (if there had been no crash). But now, I love going back. There are a lot of happy emotions too. You come to realize that life does go on, which gives us cause to celebrate and show how we can bond, how we can grow. It becomes more about celebrating life."

Family, Football and Fate

In a touching family portrait, the lasting impact of football legend Frank Loria is beautifully captured. Left to right: Victoria Buchner, the mother Phyllis Loria-Ricelli, Frank Loria Jr. and Julie Loria -- a close-knit group committed to preserving the Loria legacy. (Photo courtesy of Julie Loria)

Let me weave for you a story, one that dances between the beats of joy and sorrow, about Julie Loria and the unbreakable bond of her family. Julie's folks stand united, not just by blood, but by a profound bond of understanding and unwavering love. Every family member respects the individual quirks and traits of the other. No one ever attempts to change the other; they love each other as they are, with all their imperfections. Through sunshine and storms, they stand shoulder to shoulder.

At just 18 months old when her father passed, Julie has cultivated a profound understanding of life's delicate balance. Relationships, she points out, are precious and should never be taken for granted. "We know that life can be taken away from us any second," she said, her voice imbued with a mix of pain and wisdom. "So, we value our time together and don't waste it on anger or hate."

Among her siblings, Julie unmistakably bears a strong resemblance to her father. It's not just the facial features, or the curve of her smile or the twinkle in her eyes; it's something deeper, a certain persona she carries.

Julie credits her mother for being the bedrock of the family. Phyllis Loria-Riccelli masterfully kept Frank's memory alive while safeguarding her children from the engulfing sorrow. It was the ultimate balancing act. "My mom is such a strong woman," Julie says in a tone of admiration. "I'm sure there were some low moments. As kids, we could never tell because she hid it very well. All she ever wanted was for us to live a normal life. She found a way to put her personal feelings aside just for us."

Growing up, Julie never attended the annual fountain ceremony which honors the 75 people who perished (that was mom's decision). But all that changed once she became an adult. "It's incredibly emotional," Julie admits. "And it's so important to meet the other families who went through some very tough times. There's a strong connection that cannot be denied."

When the movie *We Are Marshall* came out, people would often approach Julie with a heavy question: *"How does that make you feel?"* Julie, who has no real-life memories of Frank Loria, would answer with grace. "As for the movie itself, I really don't have any feelings," she confessed. "But it makes me feel good to see that my dad is still so admired and loved after all these years. I talk about him being a college football star, but I also let people know that he wrote letters to his parents and to his sister about my mom and how he loved to make her happy."

The heartache of the '70 tragedy lingers, of course. And it warms Julie's heart that people continue to pay homage to the memory of her father. The most recent tribute came when Virginia Tech played a road game at Marshall in September 2023. The Hokies were given special shirts to wear as they traveled to Huntington. The schools are forever linked because two of the Herd coaches who died in the tragedy (Frank Loria and head coach Rick Tolley) played at Virginia Tech. The front of the shirt displayed Loria's name and jersey number (10); Tolley (52) was featured on the back. "These memorials for my dad make me feel really good," Julie said. "But it also hurts a little bit to think that the other beautiful souls don't have this kind of special recognition."

A Son's Yearning

In every nook and cranny of Clarksburg, the whispers of a father Frank Loria Jr. never got to embrace linger in the air. The streets singing his praises, banners of his glory days at Virginia Tech, and the annual sports awards banquet, all point towards a legendary icon. When Frank Jr. speaks of his past, the profound weight of his memories is palpable. "Despite the void," he said, "I have a lot to be thankful for. My mom is a true hero and her story is a source of strength for me. She never openly complained about the deal she was given."

As one walks through town, a sign proudly declares it the "home of Frank Loria, All-American." Further cementing Frank Sr.'s legacy is the Frank Loria Memorial Field, home for Salem University baseball, and host for the Pony League and the West Virginia state high school baseball playoffs. And let's not forget about that emblematic banner at Virginia Tech. "My dad was larger than life," says Frank Jr., his voice thick with emotion. "In my mind, he was like a superhero." Beyond the athletic fame, the son wishes to underline another facet of his father's achievements: Aside from the football exploits, Frank Loria was a two-time Academic All-America. "What I want people to realize is that Dad was able to do all this while raising a young family."

In 2000, a trip to Marshall for the unveiling of the "We Are Marshall" wall sculpture at Edwards Stadium gave Frank Jr. a broader perspective. It was his first visit, and prior to that, he knew absolutely nothing about anybody else's story except his own. All that changed once he met others whose parents died in the crash. "There's a strong bond there," he explained, "because we know how each other feels."

During the 2011 season, a touching memory was forged when Virginia Tech played a home game against Marshall. As Frank Jr. stood at midfield for the coin toss, a photograph from that day captured the moment perfectly. Reflecting on the image, Frank Jr. fondly recalled,

"I tossed that coin so high, it looks like I was looking to the heavens. That was really cool."

At Raleigh Ravenscroft (NC), Frank Jr.'s talent on the football field was evident. And he was pretty decent in high school– playing safety, running back kicks just like his dad, and he also played wingback on offense. Still, the question remained: did he have the goods to make the cut at the major-college level? Little did he know that a visit to Virginia Tech would provide some answers. As things turned out, this trip could never be viewed as typical. His father's legendary status still resonated in a powerful way.

Once Loria Jr. stepped onto the Hokies campus, it wasn't just the banners and the memories that greeted him. The warmth he felt was tangible. Virginia Tech's legendary coach, Frank Beamer, who played with Frank Jr.'s father in college, greeted him with a warmth that seemed to transcend typical recruiting gestures. Many of the assistant coaches, having been former teammates of his dad, added to this heartfelt welcome. Beamer, by the way, coached the Hokies for 29 seasons, and retired as the sixth-winningest coach in NCAA Division I Football Bowl Subdivision history.

But it was during that visit that Frank Jr. faced a revelation. "Coach Beamer told me I could try-out as a walk-on," he remembered. "Then I looked around at some of the other guys they recruited and realized that this was not about me as an individual. It was all because of my name." Then, a moment of clarity hit him, guiding him towards a path of carving his own legacy. "That's when I decided that I needed to do something different. I have to make my own life," he said. "I knew that going to West Point would make my Dad proud. Not a day goes by that I don't think about him."

As a youngster, Loria was fortunate to have constant reminders of his father's legacy and values. The memory of his dad drove him to excel in every endeavor, and to do it with integrity and goodness. He aspired to be the 'good boy' his father would have been proud of. Even as a 52-year-old man, he admits that he's a son yearning for his father's presence. While this sentiment might come across as being sad, it propels him to be the best father he can be.

Every year, Marshall University's community gathers around the
Memorial Fountain to pay homage to the 75 players, coaches,
staff and community members who lost their lives in the 1970
plane crash. (Photo courtesy of Lucianne Kautz-Call)

Over the years, Frank Jr. has visited Huntington a few times. One highlight was him being the keynote speaker for the 2005 memorial fountain ceremony, a privilege he deeply cherishes. He sees himself as an integral part of the Marshall community and hopes that the Marshall story will offer solace to those navigating adversities in their own lives.

Growing up in the shadow of a legendary father that he never knew has shaped Frank's perspectives about family and relationships.: "Because of the tragedy," he explained, "it made me want to love a little more, be accepting a little more, forgive a little more, be around people a little more."

Now, donning the hat of a father, he ensures that his children, Sophia (senior at Rutgers University), Frank III (Private First Class, US Army), Alana (3) and Malia (2), will know their grandad's story. Beyond serving in the Army and his corporate endeavors, there is no doubt about Frank Jr.'s prime purpose for his life. "Family is so important," he said emphatically. "All I want to do is take care of my wife, take care of my kids."

CHAPTER ELEVEN

50 Years & Soaring

The whispers of the past had never been louder at Marshall University. A half-century had passed since the tragic plane crash, a horrific event that profoundly reshaped the university and left a void in countless hearts. The echoing legacy of that fateful night continues to resonate, bringing forth memories, pain, and also immense pride. Walking around the Huntington campus in 2020, one was greeted by 75 hauntingly beautiful banners, each capturing a moment in time and telling a poignant tale. These banners, which will adorn the campus till spring, display the faces of individuals who may not ring a bell for every student. Still, they are undeniably the key figures who have become an indelible part of Marshall's history.

For the alumni who were there during that time, it's a journey back to yesteryears. For those folks, it's like taking a walk down memory lane and reconnecting with friends from many years ago. Yet, for the younger generation, the banners stand as an embodiment of a story – a tale of loss, grit, and the resurgence of an entire community. But the tributes didn't end there.

Thirty-nine posthumous degrees were presented by the university, honoring each student whose life was tragically cut short in the crash. With these degrees, dated with the students' expected graduation dates, Marshall paid homage not just to the players on the field, but also to the unsung heroes, from the assistant trainer to the sports editor of *The Parthenon*.

What's more, the legacy of the Young Thundering Herd and its quarterback, Reggie Oliver, continued to thrive in unique ways. Imagine driving down a street and being reminded of Reggie's enduring spirit and leadership. Well, now you can, for a street was christened in his honor, ensuring that his legacy, like those of the 75, remains deeply etched in the annals of Huntington history.

Marshall's #75 jersey was displayed in a separate showcase at the Chick-fil-A College Football Hall of Fame in recognition of the 50th anniversary of the plane crash. (Photo by Jeremy Swick/Swick Media)

The annual fountain ceremony, an emotional cornerstone for many, served as a gentle, rippling reminder of the tears shed and the spirits unbroken. To acknowledge the 50th anniversary, the Chick-fil-A

College Football Hall of Fame presented an exhibit dedicated to the '70 edition of the Thundering Herd. That display served as a heartrending reminder of how an unspeakable tragedy was transformed into a beacon of resilience and unity.

It's been said that anniversaries are a time to reflect and remember. At Marshall University, the plane crash anniversary serves as an ongoing tribute to the ones who left too soon, but will forever remain prominent in the hearts of the Thundering Herd nation.

A Street Fit for a Legend: At the crossroads of 14th Street and Charleston Avenue on Huntington's southside, there's a quiet intersection that breathes stories of an era gone by. It runs adjacent to where Fairfield Stadium once stood, echoing with the deafening roars of a crowd and the triumphant feats of players on the field. Among those gridiron legends was Marshall quarterback Reggie Oliver, who stamped his legacy on these very grounds during his college career.

Reggie Oliver, the Young Thundering Herd's iconic quarterback, has a street bearing his name. (Photo by Vic Simpson)

Now, where the iconic Fairfield Stadium once reverberated with hopes and dreams, stands a cutting-edge medical center for Marshall's School of Medicine. Yet, the past hasn't been forgotten. Right by its side, a street proudly proclaims its identity – the Honorary Reggie Oliver Square. It's not just a name on a signpost but a resounding tribute to a man who embodied tenacity and community spirit. To think, every time you cross that street, you're walking in the shadows of a legend. How incredible is that?

November 14, 1970 was an unforgettable night of devastation. Yet, from this overwhelming grief arose the Young Thundering Herd, led with unmatched fervor by Reggie Oliver. Just after the crash, there was an enduring moment that became emblematic of Reggie's leadership spirit. Mickey Jackson, former Herd assistant coach, shared a memorable story at the street-naming ceremony, one that few, if any, had heard before.

On the morning after the crash, Mickey, exhausted from a long scouting trip, got back in town around 6 a.m. Instead of heading home, he went straight to the football office. An hour later, Reggie shows up and proceeds to tell Mickey about the lengthy discussions he had with MU's freshmen players in the hours immediately following the tragedy. Reggie's determined voice spoke of an obligation to face Ohio University the following Saturday, saying, "I'm willing to bring the team out and lead us to a final victory for the year."

It's worth noting that the freshmen were indeed serious about playing the next game. But after further consideration, the decision was made to cancel the game. The grim reality was that there would still be funerals taking place throughout the country that weekend. "That's what made Reggie so special," Mickey said. "With him, it was always about leadership. Always looking ahead to the future."

If the grounds where Fairfield Stadium once rested could share their stories about Reggie Oliver, they would transport us back to Sept. 25, 1971. The atmosphere that day was thick with suspense. In the most critical moment, with the game on the line, Reggie masterfully executed the "213 Bootleg Screen," resulting in a 13-yard touchdown pass to Terry Gardner. This wasn't just a score against Xavier; it was a ray of hope, a tribute to those who perished. The emotions of the 13,000 fans from that day continue to resonate. Their collective excitement wasn't just about the game, but about healing, redemption, and the spirit of the Young Thundering Herd, beautifully reflected by Reggie Oliver.

As time marched forward, Reggie's name transformed from being a football star to being a symbol of unity, hope, and the very soul of a community. His passing in 2018, at the age of 66, left an indelible void. But in true community spirit, Huntington responded.

The ceremony to honor Reggie was nothing short of touching. Huntington Mayor Steve Williams graced the occasion, standing shoulder to shoulder with Reggie's relatives, including 93-year old Mattie Oliver Underwood, his cherished mother. Mickey Jackson, along with Red Dawson, another former Herd assistant, paid their tributes. The event was beautifully punctuated with photographic reminders displayed at the podium, each image speaking a thousand words about Reggie's unparalleled impact.

To add a unique touch to these festivities, an action figure of Reggie was also displayed, capturing the dynamism and persona of the man who once stood tall on the football field. Mickey Jackson added a lighter note, gifting Reggie's mother with the action figure and joking, "when you walk around the house, you can wave at him, or you can catch a pass from him."

Such anecdotes, both heartfelt and humorous, capture the essence of Reggie's legacy—a mix of resilience, leadership, and undying spirit. Drawing from this, it becomes more evident why Reggie's insights held such weight. He once commented on the '71 Young Thundering Herd, "All we ever wanted out of the deal was to not be forgotten. Don't ever think that we went from November 14th to winning bowl games, winning rings, and living large. Remember those people who helped put the first brick in the foundation."

In the annals of Marshall football, amidst the tales of triumph and tribulations, one spirit soars above all, unwavering and immortal—Reggie Oliver's. His legacy, his passion, and his dedication resonate through the ages, a testament that will never fade. Indeed, Reggie Oliver is not just a memory; he is the very heartbeat of Thundering Herd football.

0

Fountain's Timeless Roar: There was an uncanny touch of déjà vu when November 14, 2020, landed on a Saturday, mirroring the same weekday from 50 years ago. The Fountain Ceremony has always served as a beacon of remembrance. But the 50th edition? Well, it had an all-together different flavor.

2020 dawned as a year clouded by the shadow of the COVID-19 pandemic, leading to the cancellation of countless events. Still, Marshall's annual tribute continued. This particular ceremony was an exclusive, invitation-only event. Imagine a gathering of devoted attendees, their expressions concealed behind facemasks, standing six feet apart — the poignant image of our new reality. Even with the mandated health measures in place, the heart and soul of the ceremony remained intact.

Scanning the crowd, all you could see was a mini-herd of folks wearing vibrant kelly green, that unmistakable Marshall hue. You also saw swirls of inky black interspersed here and there. But, wait a sec! Your eyes can't help but notice four elderly gents decked out in purple and gold. Now you wonder, who are these guys? Well, let's time-travel back to '70! Say hello to Grover Truslow, Richard Peeler, Chuck Zadnik and Rusty Scales. These fellas played for East Carolina in a nail-biter of a game against Marshall that the Pirates won 17-14.

But, here's the twist. These gentlemen didn't come to town to rekindle old glories. Nah, they were on a heartfelt mission. To bow their heads and remember. Think about it: playing an adrenaline-pumping game and then finding out the team you just played was involved in such a devastating tragedy. That's heavy stuff, real heavy. Even if you weren't directly hit by the blow, the ripple effects of such news can still put you in a daze. Man, that stuff sticks with you forever. The horror, the disbelief – it was crystal clear in their minds.

So clear, in fact, that the East Carolina coaching staff held a 2 a.m. memorial service. That's just hours after the crash, folks. Imagine the raw emotions among the players at both schools. Their fates are intertwined, their histories forever linked by that shared heartbreak. That's why these former East Carolina players wanted to be there, standing in solidarity, remembering. And perhaps there was some healing. They all laid a rose at the fountain during the ceremony.

As the Fountain Ceremony unfolded, it remained an emotionally charged event. A representative from Ceredo-Kenova first responders, alongside Marshall's head football coach (Doc Holliday at that time), ceremoniously placed a wreath at the front of the fountain. This is a solemn occasion to pay tribute. A time for reflection. A time to realize that even though life doesn't always go as planned, it's still worth living.

Now, imagine Lucianne Kautz-Call at the podium. Her connection with Marshall University is not just as a graduate, former cheerleader and a 15-year member of the ceremony planning committee. It's personal. Her father, Charles Kautz, Marshall's athletic director in '70, was among those lost in the crash. She remembers the harrowing day he went to work and never returned. "I never got the chance to say goodbye," she said, her voice dripping with nostalgia and grief.

But Lucianne's eyes light up every time she dives into the Marshall tale. To her, it's not just any story; it's a thrilling saga of resilience. Can you believe Marshall rebuilt from almost nothing, rising like a phoenix to become the gold standard for epic comebacks?

Towards the end of her keynote speech, she held a Marshall football helmet high, and the energy in the audience was electric! The crowd roared back in unity, their voices echoing: "We Are Marshall! We Are Marshall! We Are Marshall!" Now, doesn't that give you chills?

Kautz-Call's life-long love affair with Marshall gives her a unique perspective that few can match. "The spirit and unity of Marshall and the community has always been strong," she asserted. "The tragedy simply brought everybody closer together." Although it took more than a decade for the program to find its competitive footing, Kautz-Call points to Marshall's scintillating win over Xavier in '71 as a benchmark moment. "That's when the healing process started to take place," she said.

Fast forward another 28 years and the process comes full circle as the Herd closes out the decade of the '90s with the winningest record in NCAA Division I football. Definitely a shining example of a once-floundering program going from the worst to first. "Ending the '90s like that was the grand finale as far as I'm concerned," she said with a gleam in her eye. "That's when the dream we lost with the 75 (who died) was finally fulfilled."

Looking back over those memorable five decades, Kautz-Call's belief is stronger than ever. The echoes of the tragedy and its teachings are undeniable. "God gives us this life," she shared, "and every day is important. So, take the life you have and use it to the best of your ability."

In commemoration of the 50th anniversary of the Marshall plane crash, Jeremy Swick designed a special exhibit that was featured prominently in the Chick-fil-A College Football Hall of Fame. (Photo by Jeremy Swick/Swick Media)

Hall of Fame Exhibit: For years, living comfortably in Fayetteville, Georgia, a mere 30 miles from Atlanta's bustling streets, Debbie (Bailey) Bowen held a quiet conviction. She was certain that the Chick-fil-A

College Football Hall of Fame would undoubtedly commemorate the '70 plane crash and the poignant stories woven around it.

While the cacophony of Atlanta's crowds and its notorious traffic never appealed to her, 2020 was different. It marked the 50th anniversary of the tragedy. Feeling the weight of the occasion, Debbie steeled herself, deciding that now was the time to deal with the city's chaos and finally see the tribute she believed was there. But instead of a heartfelt homage, she was met with a stark revelation that shook her to the core.

"I was so sure Marshall's legacy would be there," Debbie admitted, her voice tinged with disbelief. She soon learned that many had asked questions about a Marshall exhibit, only to receive the same, perplexing answer: "We don't have one." No one could explain this glaring omission.

Not one to back down, Debbie, MU's first black cheerleader, jumped in with both feet and embarked on a mission. She crafted a meticulous proposal, painting the poignant story of the crash, its profound effect on the school, and the community's heartbreak. Her words flowed like a riveting news piece. How could the Hall of Fame not have known about this epic tale?

Despite the challenges posed by the COVID-19 pandemic, by late autumn, her sticktoitiveness bore fruit. Jeremy Swick, the Hall's curator and historian at the time, designed an awe-inspiring exhibit, composed of eight panels, each focusing on an aspect of the tragedy. Yes!!!! The Herd made it to the Hall! "I wanted the world to understand that this wasn't just about football," Swick shared, his voice brimming with passion about the exhibit. "It was about an entire community—players, coaches, cheerleaders, boosters—each with a story of its own."

The homage didn't end with that one exhibit. Marshall's story was prominently displayed on the marquee billboard at the Hall's primary entrance on Marietta Street in downtown Atlanta. The building glowed in verdant hues, crowned by the haunting number 75 on the front wall, a tribute to those who lost their lives on the night of the crash. Also, a #75 Marshall jersey was displayed in a separate showcase along with other historical memorabilia such as one of Coach Nick Saban's jackets at Alabama and the #16 jersey worn by Trevor Lawrence when he played at Clemson.

Debbie's heart swelled with pride, "This is a part of sports history," she exclaimed, "and now, everyone who steps into the Hall of Fame will know Marshall's legacy." For a fleeting moment, everything felt right. Marshall's '70 team had finally received the recognition it deserved. But, as in all compelling tales, there is a twist. The joy and excitement was short-lived. As things turned out, the exhibit was only temporary and it lasted a mere three weeks. "I couldn't believe it," Debbie sighed, "Three weeks? Why not permanently?"

Hall of Fame officials told Debbie that a permanent display for Marshall might set a precedent, obliging them to do the same for others. *"Wait a minute,"* Debbie thought. Upon researching, she found out about four tragedies involving college football teams, none of which came close to the magnitude of Marshall's loss. To further underscore this point, Wichita State, one of those four, doesn't even participate in football any longer.

Seeking clarity, I personally approached Hall of Fame representatives. The official stance? "No plans at this time" to grant Marshall a permanent space. However, they did hint at possibly adding Marshall to the digital timeline which highlights significant events since the dawn of college football in 1869. So, where does Marshall stand out in this history?

In '71, Marshall was given permission by the NCAA to let freshmen participate in varsity football, a step that was unprecedented at the time. This wasn't just a "special exemption." This proved to be a testament to the indomitable spirit of Marshall. Getting a mere mention in a timeline does not truly capture the essence of the Herd's journey. Doesn't even come close.

So, does that mean the battle for recognition is over? Far from it. Skeptical about whether Marshall's Thundering Herd deserves a permanent spot? Dive into the next chapter and discover the compelling reasons why.

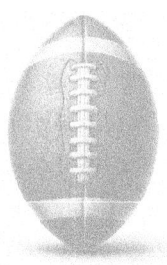

CHAPTER TWELVE

The Case for the Herd in the Hall

When you think of incredible comebacks, tales of insurmountable odds, and pure, never-say-die tenacity, Marshall University's football journey should be front and center. It's a narrative not just of talent and skill, but of heart, soul, and resilience that's unparalleled in collegiate history. There's no denying that the Thundering Herd's odyssey, from ground zero to soaring pinnacles, belongs in the Chick-fil-A College Football Hall of Fame.

To understand the magnitude of Marshall's sojourn, you need a bit of context. Just prior to the tragic crash in '70, which claimed the lives of 75 souls, the football team had not had a winning season in six years. The shadow of defeat hung heavily over the program, leading many to ask: Why not just give up on football? Especially when the basketball team was blazing trails and had a Top 20 national ranking. Heck, back in 1955, Marshall made history by signing Hal Greer, the first black scholarship athlete to attend a public college in West Virginia. That's the same Hal Greer who was immortalized in the Naismith Basketball Hall of Fame and hailed as one of the Top 50 Greatest Players in NBA History.

But walking away from adversity and throwing hands up in the air, is not in Marshall's DNA. This is a school that forged a reputation for staring challenges in the face and rising to the occasion.

In the immediate aftermath of the plane crash, the '70s painted a bleak picture. Marshall's football team was among the nation's worst.

Yet, in a twist that feels straight out of a Hollywood script, by the end of the '90s, the team finished with the best winning percentage in all of NCAA football. Talk about a phoenix rising!

And while the crash was undeniably the darkest chapter in Marshall's history, the program's ability to bounce back was tested even before that. Cast your mind back two years prior, when the university was slammed with over 100 recruiting violations. NCAA probation followed swiftly. As if that wasn't enough, Marshall was kicked out of the Mid-American Conference. As for the stadium? Far from state-of-the-art. The summer of '69 was a nightmare - a scandal that started with an undefeated freshman team ready to take over, only to see the dreams shatter, coaches get fired, players leave, and a roster slashed in half.

But this is where the true essence of Marshall University emerges. Many would have seen this series of unfortunate events as a sign to abandon ship. Not Marshall, which displayed an audacious, gutsy spirit to keep the football program alive. This isn't just a story of athletic achievement. It's a testament to the human spirit of a school and community that never gave up. Every win Marshall notches, every championship it claims, every bowl victory it celebrates, is a continuation of a story that began in the depths of despair, but rose to unprecedented heights. The evidence shouts that the Marshall story is not just a footnote in history.

The College Football Hall of Fame isn't just about enshrining winning records or legendary athletes. It's about honoring the spirit of the game. And few stories embody that spirit like Marshall University. The time has come for Marshall to claim its rightful place among football's most iconic stories, a permanent space where generations can bear witness to the tale of a team that redefined resilience. A space where every visitor will be reminded that even when faced with the darkest night, there's always the promise of a new dawn. Let Marshall's light shine brighter than ever. And that's because legends ... they're forever.

Debbie (Bailey) Bowen played a key role in making sure that Marshall got a temporary display in the Chick-Fil-A College Football Hall of Fame during the 50th anniversary of the '70 plane crash. (Photo courtesy of Chief Justice Yearbook/Marshall University)

CHAPTER THIRTEEN

Media's Spin on Marshall Disaster

The breathtaking tale of Marshall University football's comeback is one for the history books. Imagine this: a team on the brink of being erased from existence due to a nightmarish plane crash. Yet, the school, fueled by sheer determination, refuses to drop the ball on football. As they painstakingly rebuilt, the Thundering Herd journeyed from near obliteration to the limelight. It's a narrative that's nothing short of invigorating and inspiring.

For a whopping thirty years, this incredible saga sat in the shadows, waiting for its deserved spotlight. Finally, the silence ended in 2000 with documentaries like *Ashes to Glory* and *Remembering Marshall.* Following these was another doc, *Return of the Thundering Herd,* and then a book, *The Marshall Story.*

So, why the wait? It wasn't for lack of interest. The heart of the matter lay with the painful memories and the desperate need to handle the story with grace and respect. Those most intimate with the tragedy often found it heart-wrenching to relive those days, making it difficult to move forward with media portrayals. And while the story was decades in the making, Marshall football's crowning moment didn't come till the late '90s. By the close of '99, the Herd was the talk of the town, ranking at No. 10 nationally and closing out the decade as the winningest program in NCAA Division I.

Surprise spotlight: Images of the author (like the one above)
appeared unexpectedly multiple times in the documentary
Ashes to Glory. (Photo: Herald-Dispatch)

Ashes to Glory and *Remembering Marshall* provided gripping personal accounts from survivors, friends, and families of the victims. These documentaries, released on the thirtieth anniversary of the crash, provided an eye-opening glimpse into the night of the tragedy and the aftermath. Then came the *Return of the Thundering Herd* documentary, setting the stage for the movie *We Are Marshall*. This film, backed by highly-regarded Warner Bros., reached millions, raking in about $33 million in just 20 days. And let's not forget its numerous runs as a TV feature and DVD sales.

The hoopla around *We Are Marshall* was electric. It was a nostalgic trip down memory lane for many Marshall alumni, sparking memories and uniting old friends. Discussions blossomed everywhere: phone calls, emails, and online messages were buzzing. And me? I never dreamed that I'd write a book. I was more of a newspaper and magazine kinda guy. But everything changed in 2000. And while I never made it into any documentaries or movies about Marshall's past, the events of that year tied me to it in a unique way.

When ESPN approached me about appearing in a segment of their documentary, *Remembering Marshall,* I was shocked. Although the segment never materialized, it's mind-blowing to think of how much interest there was in hearing my two cents worth.

My outlook on my connection to Thundering Herd football took a 180-degree turn after I watched *Ashes to Glory* for the first time. This Emmy Award-winning documentary had been out for nearly a year and I knew absolutely nothing about it. All that changed when I returned to Marshall for homecoming weekend in 2001, my first homecoming visit in almost twenty years. I was in town for maybe ninety minutes when Vic Simpson, a longtime friend and college buddy, handed me a videotape. My gaze was fixed on the cassette's title, written with a black felt-tip marker. Vic left me hanging, choosing not to divulge the contents of the tape, letting anticipation build up within me.

Vic's voice carried a hint of intrigue. "Taped this the other night. You're gonna wanna see this."

My curiosity piqued, I asked, "What is it?"

Vic's response stirred more intrigue. "Herd football in 1970 and you're in it."

Incredulity was evident in my response. "Naaaaaaah. That couldn't be. *You know* I didn't play ball that year."

Unfazed, Vic retorted with assurance. "Yeah, I know. Like I said, you're gonna wanna see this." His words reverberated in my head, heightening my interest in the mysterious tape.

So, after spending one night at Marshall's Homecoming, I drove back to North Carolina the next day to cover a college football game that night. A few days later, I carved out some time to watch the video for the first time, intrigued by what this unexpected gift from Vic might hold. Now, mind you, I hadn't even heard of *Ashes to Glory*, even though it had been out for a year. I anticipated a documentary related to the Herd, but what I got was a shocking revelation.

Pop in the tape, and there's a segment showcasing key defensive players from the '70 season. First up – Felix Jordan. But lo and behold, it's not him—it's me! There I am, donning my old jersey number, 21. Oh, the irony! After I left the team, Felix played my position and got my old number. But the kicker? Repeatedly, there I am, on the screen. It's like watching a ghost from the past.

Now, here's the part that sends chills down my spine every single time. Rick Meckstroth remembers the moments before the tragic crash. Then the narrator mentions Felix not being on the plane because he was pulled off the team bus to make room for a booster who helped pay for the cost of the plane trip. Guess whose picture they splash across the screen? Yours truly! I feel the weight of it. It's surreal. Had I chosen to play just one more year, I could've been on that ill-fated flight. How wild is that?

At the *Ashes to Glory* premier, the mix-up didn't slide under the radar. Former players Ed Carter and Reggie Oliver, both integral to the documentary, were abuzz about the glaring oversight. But this wasn't a quick fix. Several months passed before the DVD edition appeared, and when it did, they amended the blunder – supplanting my images with Felix's. Ever wondered how such an oversight can happen? Blame it on budget constraints and the mammoth task of working through a maze of unlabeled photos.

Ya' know what's really bizarre? I recognized all those photos shown in the doc. My younger self, working part-time at the *Herald-Dispatch* sports department, had flipped through all those images years ago. It's amazing how vividly I remember them – crop marks and all. And that's my slice of life – a tape that wasn't just about football, but a poignant reminder of the fragility of life and destiny's unpredictable turns.

When tragedy struck, Bill Dodson was lost in its dark embrace. It's not every day you come face to face with such an overwhelming heartbreak. "I did not have any sense of closure," he admitted, his voice a whisper of raw emotion, years of buried pain echoing from the past. For Bill D, watching *Ashes to Glory* was like turning on a light in a long-darkened room. Suddenly, everything was illuminated. "After viewing the film," he explained, "I had more perspective on the crash and felt compelled to reconnect with Marshall." Dodson did so in a significant way, launching an initiative in Nate Ruffin's name. The initiative aimed to increase black alumni support for the school's $100-million campaign.

As for the movie, the very beginning should have alerted viewers that there would be some distortions of what actually happened. At the top of the screen in big, bold letters, it read: . "This is a true story." *We Are Marshall* promises truth, but sometimes, Hollywood weaves its own narrative. While the movie might not have been a mirror reflection of reality, for those haunted by the memories of November 14, it was an agonizing revisitation. Albert Evans, his voice tinged with pain from yesteryears, confessed, "I can't even watch it. Every time it comes on, I start crying."

Another tale from this woven tapestry is Ed Carter. A beacon in the real-life Marshall story, you won't find him in the movie. Why is he absent? It's by design, not by accident. "I didn't believe it was in the Lord's will for me to be in a production with profanity," Ed shared. Yet, a character, unspoken but familiar, makes his presence felt (without speaking) in a few scenes – an Afro-ed, muscular player wearing jersey number 77, a silent homage to Ed. "It's not just about the profanity," Ed clarifies. "I might watch it at some point. But for now, I just haven't made the choice."

But Ed isn't the only no-show in the flick. Felix Jordan, another figure who is forever linked with the '70 Herd, is conspicuously absent. Warner Bros. tried, oh how they tried, to ink his story into the script, but Felix? He remained a closed book. "I wouldn't have signed away my rights," he shared, firm in his stance.

In the days leading up to the movie's nationwide premier, Felix's voice rang on my phone line after thirty-something years. *We Are Marshall* was creating waves, ripples of excitement. But Felix? He wavered, a mix of anticipation and apprehension. As things turned out, he opted to attend a special showing of the movie with a group of former Xavier players that he played against in '71. "I was thinking about not going because I wasn't sure how I might react," Felix confessed, the weight of history on his shoulders. As the credits faded and the theater grew silent, he shared "It wasn't as bad as I thought it would be."

Through the cinematic lens, *We Are Marshall* is more than just a movie. It's memories, grief, hope, and a journey – both personal and collective – for those connected to Marshall's legacy. The film plunges you deep into the heartbreak that gripped the Marshall campus and its surrounding community. The raw emotion is palpable. You feel the weight of the loss; it's like a dense fog. And let's give a nod to the filmmakers here: they made a choice that was a breath of fresh air. Rather than making it another gridiron epic, it's more about rising from the ashes, about conquering life's darkest moments. It's not just about touchdowns and victories.

But, oh my goodness, let's talk about some snags.

You've got these central figures, right? Paul Griffen, whose son tragically died in the crash; Annie Cantrell, the love left behind; and Tom Bogdan, Nate Ruffin's roommate, who fatefully overslept that fateful day and never boarded that doomed flight. The weight of survivor's guilt was so intense for Tom that he couldn't bring himself to lace up those cleats ever again. They could've been compelling figures driving the story. Except for one glaring hiccup: these folks? Pure invention. They never existed.

What bums me out further is that the film barely scratches the surface on the real-life heroes of the '70 team. Like, did you know that Art Harris and Ted Shoebridge were basically the golden boys of college recruiting? Or that there were these four groundbreaking players from Alabama, pioneers in their families to attend college?

And here's another head-scratcher. There's this scene, right, where suddenly there's this "aha!" moment to switch Reggie Oliver from wide receiver to quarterback. Spoiler: that's just Hollywood jibber-jabber. Reggie had been a star QB since his high school days in Alabama. Though he split time between playing quarterback and wide receiver during '71 spring practice, he never played wide-out after that. Reggie was a full-time quarterback for the rest of his playing career.

While I'm on the subject, let's dive a bit deeper on Reggie. During the racially-sensitive early '70s, discovering black quarterbacks at mainstream schools was as rare as spotting polar bears in Panama. Reggie, even before the likes of legends like Doug Williams, Warren Moon and Randall Cunningham, was a trailblazer. He wasn't just any QB; he was one of the rising stars in the World Football League before it folded due to financial problems.

Transitioning from Reggie's groundbreaking presence to the film's dramatic conclusion, let's discuss the movie's defining moment. The climactic game-winning play is more Hollywood magic than reality. Sure, in real life, the Herd clinched victory with a last-second pass, but the details? Miles off. The movie shows us a scrambling Reggie chucking the ball to Terry Gardner in the end zone. It's flashy, sure. But that's no screen pass. And the real Gardner? Running? Yes. Spectacular catches? Not his forte. In reality, the ending was far more gripping than this cinematic rendition.

Imagine if, just for a moment, you were thrust into a heart-stopping scene straight from a nail-biting movie: Everything's slowed down, the background noise fades, and the world focuses on one critical, electric moment. That's how it felt in real life when Gardner caught that screen pass in the Xavier game. There was a blocker in position, and just one defender in his way. Honestly, Terry could've waltzed past him even if they were playing tag or flag football. Pure gridiron poetry.

We Are Marshall is one of those underdog stories that grabs your heart and doesn't let go. And while I'm all for a cinematic masterpiece, it's just a shame that they didn't let the story speak for itself. The real events? Absolutely riveting. No need for any Hollywood seasoning here. I've read the reviews, combed through the articles, and I still scratch my head. Why change the story when it's already gold? Sure, they say, "It's all about capturing the essence," but why not just label the film "based on a true story?" At least then we'd know where we stand.

And let me tell you, I'm not alone. I've been on the phone, exchanged endless emails, and the consensus among my old pals? The movie missed a beat or three. Dickie Carter put it plainly, "The movie was off-kilter from the jump. Coach Tolley would've never let his players mess around after a loss."

By the way, if you bring it up with Chuck Landon, be prepared. The Marshall graduate turned astute sports columnist has consistently pointed out how the film not only took extensive creative liberties, but also butchered the truth in the process. For example, the film got it all twisted in its portrayal of Coach Red Dawson. Chuck only watched *We Are Marshall* once, and I can't blame him. He told me, "All I wanted was for them to get it right, to honor those we lost. Instead, they played us a fairy tale."

Now, here's a kicker for you: Terry Gardner, the hero of our story, didn't even get to see the film. He passed away a few months before its debut. And rumor has it, if he hadn't given his blessing, we might've seen a completely different character, named Billy Bob, making that iconic touchdown. Talk about a detour from reality!

You see, Hollywood has a knack for tweaking tales. Remember *The Express*, the movie about Ernie Davis, the first black Heisman Trophy winner? Well, his teammates weren't too thrilled with the "creative liberties" taken. One of them, Ger Schwedes, even penned a letter, stating, "The movie is a fiction masterpiece. But it's not our story."

So, while *We Are Marshall* has its merits, let's not forget the real heroes and their true, incredible journey.

Reading a column in a North Carolina newspaper about the *We Are Marshall* premiere sparked a flaming desire in me to share my narrative. The piece highlighted Jim Grobe, then the head football coach at Wake Forest University. When I learned that Grobe grew up in Huntington, West Virginia, my level of interest escalated.

See, Grobe wasn't at Marshall during the tragedy, but he was around, being a college student elsewhere. His connection was deep, yet not personal. For his wife Holly, the air in Huntington was thick with grief in '70. Every time she heard the name Kathy Heath, her childhood friend, her heart weighed a thousand pounds. Kathy had lost both parents in the crash, both were avid supporters of Marshall athletics.

Now, picture me reflecting on my own memories of the crash, sipping tea and tracing back the years. Grobe and I, though different, were intertwined by the same historical threads. Oddly enough, I unintentionally diminished the value of my own voice and experiences, compared to those of others. Then there was that unexpected, really weird encounter at Wal-Mart. Picture this huge bin stuffed with DVDs of every sort of movie you can think of. I had been scanning the titles, particularly intrigued by a few about Marshall, when a stranger approached. No introductions, no pleasantries, just a connection over a shared, albeit distinct, past.

This guy described a haunting scene: Tri-State Airport, a week after the tragedy, with the twisted wreckage from the crash and the scorched landscape reminiscent of a devastating forest fire. As he spoke, the world faded. It felt like I was airborne, glimpsing the terrain of Huntington from a plane window, the memories rushing back as if it was just yesterday. Strange, isn't it? The threads of the past weaving seamlessly with the present.

Moved and motivated by all this, I reached out to local media. Hoping to share my story, my experiences. And while I initially considered TV, the allure of the written word was too strong. So, I met with sports editor Terri Oberle of the *Winston-Salem Journal,* graphically recounting my days at Marshall. Teri listened intently. To my surprise, instead of assigning a writer to interview me, Terri threw me a split-fingered fastball. "You write it," he said, "let the world know your perspective."

But reality isn't always kind, is it? Despite my optimism, the days turned into weeks, weeks into months, and months into a full year. My story, still wrapped in the confines of a drawer. See, I knew the drill. Priorities. The newspaper had its favorites - ACC football and basketball, stock car racing, and high schools. My story, despite its worthiness, was just a whisper among roaring headlines.

Eventually, I decided to let it go, thanking Terri for the opportunity. My story needed its own space, a platform where it could breathe, unfettered by restrictions. And so, from the embers of that unshared narrative, my memoir was born, recounting the Marshall plane crash and its profound aftermath. Sometimes, it's not just about the story, but the journey it takes to find its voice.

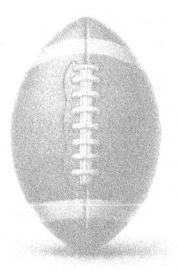

CHAPTER FOURTEEN

Bits & Bites

After my first memoir was published, the enlightening feedback from readers spoke volumes. So, here's a "this and that" chapter—a mosaic of lesser-known tales and tidbits. If the original memoir was a delicious main course, this is the tantalizing seasoning that elevates every bite.

These aren't just stories; they're uncharted territories in an already rich landscape. Ready for the journey? Then dig in!

Bill, Gaylord & Alex Haley

Remember that earlier chapter about the Homegoing Caravan and how it was put together? There's a juicy tidbit I left out – a little "by the way" for you to think about. Now, amidst all our reminiscing about the days following the crash, a certain interaction between two energetic dudes slipped right past my radar. Yep, I'm talking about schoolmates Bill Dodson and Gaylord Stewart, and their rendezvous with Alex Haley.

Wait, *the* Alex Haley? The one who'd later craft *Roots*? Indeed, the same!

Here's how it went down. Marshall's black students are convening at the "Bus Station," a few nights after the crash. Mostly everyone is there, deep in discussion and reflection, when Gaylord drops a nugget. He says, "Bill, there's this speaker at Old Main Auditorium who's doing some deep research on slavery. Should we check it out?" At this point, it's essential to note that while *Roots* was still a few years away in Haley's repertoire, he had already made waves with his bestseller, *The Autobiography of Malcolm X*.

Bill, ever the inquisitive one, looks at Gaylord and nods, "Let's go!" So, they head over to Old Main. There, they find themselves face-to-face with Mr. Haley. With their signature blend of respect and curiosity, Bill and Gaylord initiate a conversation, explaining why no black students attended his lecture. So, what does Haley do? With that characteristic thoughtful expression, he says, "How about I join your meeting?"

Now, pause for a second: A bestselling author, the name behind one of the defining books of our era, just wanting to stop by our little gathering? That, my friends, is how legends roll!

So here's to Bill and Gaylord – who remind us that sometimes, in the most unsuspecting of moments, history reveals its wonders. Cheers!

Ode to the Silver Screen

The Henson & Kitchen Mortuary in Huntington, West Virginia has a unique lounge area that showcases memorabilia from the '70 Thundering Herd and the movie *We Are Marshall*. (Photo courtesy of Fred Kitchen)

Imagine stepping into a funeral home only to find yourself wrapped in the embrace of Hollywood history. Welcome to Henson & Kitchen Mortuary (Huntington, West Virginia), where the aura is a mix of somberness and cinematic nostalgia. Every nook and corner of the lounge area dazzles with treasures dedicated to the '70 Thundering Herd football team. The memorabilia sprawled around isn't just some fine artistry – it's the real deal, artifacts used in the 2006 movie, *We Are Marshall*.

The mortuary's Life and Legacy Cafe has been a cornerstone of reflection and tribute since 2012. So ... how did Fred Kitchen, owner of the mortuary, manage to get his hands on these items? It's a fun tale. The movie bigwigs at Warner Brothers needed an authentic casket for a rain scene. Enter Fred's then-business, Batesville Casket Company, with a pristine mahogany casket ready for its close-up. However, Mother Nature had other plans! A shower and a misstep later, the beautiful casket lay in the grave, looking a little worse for wear. But instead of a sad ending, this casket found a new home – in Fred's basement.

Roll the tape forward, and today that same casket is a conversation piece in a heart-warming exhibit, all thanks to Fred's decision to buy Henson Mortuary in 2010. And if you're wondering about the origins of the other exhibit treasures, Fred connected with the Marshall University Foundation, who gave him the iconic jersey from the film and several relics. Kitchen obliged by making a donation to the foundation.

"The response has grown over the years,"Kitchen beamed, "but we're finding out that a lot of people in town still don't know about it." Fred's collection doesn't just stop at a jersey and a casket. He has a myriad of pieces from the movie – shirts, bags, call sheets, even the director's chair! There's a script, handwritten notes, and so much more. Rumor has it, there are still undiscovered gems hiding within the folds of that famous casket.

The doors of this mortuary-museum swing open every weekday. While word of this enchanting exhibit continues to spread, Fred's intent isn't to merely showcase. He wants visitors to feel, relive, and reminisce. "People are always blown away when they come in," he said. "We're the only ones (funeral homes) who do this."

Frozen in Time

When the '70 Herd comes to mind, it's impossible not to visualize the serene grounds of the Marshall University campus. But let's not be mistaken, Huntington's embrace is just a fraction of the vast tapestry of love and memory woven for those who were lost.

The four Alabama players who died in the '70 plane crash have been immortalized with a permanent exhibit at the Warner Transportation Center Museum in Tuscaloosa. (Photo courtesy of the Warner Transportation Museum)

Blink back to 2012, in Tuscaloosa, Alabama – not just a football town, but a place where memories of Larry Sanders, Joe Hood, Robert VanHorn, and Freddy Wilson find a sacred resting place. These four spirits, once vibrant students of Druid High School, are immortalized in a permanent exhibit at the Warner Transportation Museum. Imagine walking through those corridors, where the echo of their laughter

The unveiling ceremony at the museum was a ballet of emotions. Imagine a somber gathering where families' eyes shimmered with tears of both anguish and honor.

lingers, only to be hushed by the melancholic reality of the plane crash that stole them from this world.

Although they're no longer with us, their aspirations to be honored in the Alabama Sports Hall of Fame remains. With each passing year, the Tuscaloosa City Council stands firm, with the belief that these names will eventually be etched on the Hall's walls.

The unveiling ceremony at the museum was a ballet of emotions. Imagine a somber gathering where families' eyes shimmered with tears of both anguish and honor. City officials stood erect, and coaches – including Kenneth O'Rourke who had coached the four departed players at Druid and previously served as the freshman coach at Marshall – reflected on their days with the athletes. Former Marshall assistants Mickey Jackson and Carl Kokor, shared their sentiments as well. Kenneth's voice, imbued with a mix of grief and fervor, harmonized with the insights of Kokor and Jackson, weaving a tapestry of memories so vivid, it felt as though time had rewound.

Now, pivot your gaze to the north. Rutherford, New Jersey – a town, like Tuscaloosa, that feels a heartache so profound. The Meadowlands Museum, in 2014, threw open its doors to welcome the memories of Marcel Lajterman, Ted Shoebridge, Kevin Gilmore, and Art Harris. Although this was a temporary display it wasn't merely a showcase; it was an embrace. Plaques shimmered with the reflection of their youthful aspirations, and passionate speeches seemed to breathe life into their stories, ensuring that their flame of legacy never flickers out.

As the years roll on in Tuscaloosa and Rutherford, life's relentless march doesn't blur these stories. Instead, it magnifies them, engraving them deeper into the hearts of these communities.

CRAIG T. GREENLEE

Board named to hold hearing on plane crash

By CRAIG T. GREENLEE
Staff reporter

A four-man board of inquiry has been named to conduct a federal hearing here Dec. 14 into the Nov. 14 airplane crash that took the lives of 75 persons, including most of the MU football team, several coaches, officials, and supporters.

Edward Slattery, director of the office of public affairs of the National Transportation Safety Board, told The Parthenon Tuesday from his Washington office that the hearing panel would include Oscar Laurel, NTSB member and presiding officer; assistant, C. O. Miller, director of the Bureau of Aviation Safety; Richard Rodriguez, hearing officer; and David Zimmermann from the office of general council.

Members of the board of inquiry were selected by John Reed, NTSB chairman, according to Slattery.

"This panel will listen to testimony and other information concerning the accident and will then return to Washington and have all the information analyzed by the NTSB. Then the long drawn out process of the completing the final report will begin," said Slattery.

"It will take a while to give the results of the findings of the board because the process is extremely thorough and very meticulous. I don't expect that the findings of the board be completed before April."

In discussing witnesses that will be questioned at the hearing, Slattery said, "a list of the witnesses will not be released until the morning of the hearing," he said.

"Anyone who thinks that they may know something that may be of help will have to contact Richard Rodriguez in Washington, in order that their testimony may be heard."

Officials are trying to pinpoint whether instrument failure or pilot misjudgement caused the chartered DC9 jet to clip the treetops of a darkened ridge on a low approach at night to an airport obscured by rain.

The NTSB is expected to hear 20 witnesses, including its own technical experts, during the three-day session.

The Marshall team was flying back from East Carolina Nov. 14 when its chartered Southern Airways jet hit the ridge, crashed into a nearby hillside, and exploded. There were no survivors.

Author's front-page article about the federal investigation of the plane crash was published in *The Parthenon,* the school's student newspaper.

186

Ceremony Critique Sparks Outrage

The year was 2012, when everyone was probably trying to perfect the Gangnam Style dance. Meanwhile, Marshall student Henry Culvyhouse, took a bold leap into the world of journalism. In *The Parthenon*, the school's student newspaper, he penned a provocative editorial titled "Time Heals All Wounds." Now, this wasn't your standard "Oops, I accidentally texted my crush instead of my best friend" goof, but more of an "Oops, I tried to do the Harlem Shake and knocked over grandma's vase" level of klutzmanship.

For whatever reason, our friend Henry decided that the 42nd anniversary of the plane crash was the perfect moment to put his clear-sightedness on public display. What came out in print was pure disaster. He wrote: "Forty-two years have passed, why must we continue to be reminded?"And then, adding some extra spice to his take, he compared the somber memorial ceremony to festive times like Thanksgiving or Christmas. Henry, my dude, that's like comparing chalk to cheese... or turkey to tofu!

The digital realm erupted faster than a cheetah on the chase. Students, alumni, and anyone with a keyboard turned into instant critics. Among the horde was Randy Burnside, dropping wisdom like it was hot: "Kid, you just do not get it." Preach, Randy! He reminded everyone that the crash was one thing, but the resilience and spirit of Marshall's response? Now that's legendary.

But this episode didn't end there. Henry was summoned to air out his laundry on a radio talk show. They didn't exactly roll out the red carpet. Woody Woodrum, one of the hosts, humorously mentioned his 76-year-old mother was keen on setting Henry straight. Yikes! Granny's wrath is a force to reckon with. Henry, to his credit, wasn't entirely tone-deaf. He admitted he might've been a bit...heavy-handed in his choice of words. And as Thanksgiving loomed, he hinted at making an early exit. Probably wise, given that he'd ruffled enough feathers without involving an actual turkey.

And thus, in the grand annals of 2012, alongside dance crazes and fashion faux pas, we add Henry's lesson: Think before you type. And maybe, keep your holiday comparisons away from sensitive topics. Three cheers for hindsight!

Three Takes About the Chant

Remember the chant in the movie *We Are Marshall*? Remember how the chant was portrayed as the lifeline of the Marshall community after the plane crash? The thing is, the chant wasn't historically accurate for that time. As for the passion, the strength, and the unity it conveyed ... that was real. Three stories—those of Carol Richardson McCullough, Woody Woodrum and Nate Ruffin as recounted by Robert Walker— tell us why.

- Carol Richardson McCullough —Marshall cheerleader in the early '70s, clears up some misconceptions. No, the chant did not exist during the time of the crash. But she personally vouched for its authenticity soon after. "We DID use that cheer as early as 1973." She paints a clear image of cheerleaders clapping and chanting

  "We Are (clap-clap) Mar-shall (clap-clap)"
  "We Are (clap-clap) Mar-shall (clap-clap)"

- Woody Woodrum — Longtime on-air personality acknowledges the inaccuracies about the chant in the film. That chant, as done in the movie, said Woodruff, didn't start until the mid-80s at Fairfield Stadium. "Then it really took off in '91," he said. "The scoreboard at the new stadium would show flashing arrows, which prompted each side as to what part of the chant to shout." Woody, however, gives us an insightful reminder about the subject. "We are... Marshall!" isn't just about a chant. It's about an undying spirit.

- Robert Walker, a Marshall graduate, takes us on a journey, giving us a precious memory from Nate Ruffin (former MU player who didn't make the plane trip because of an injury). Picture this: 1999, in the intimidating "Death Valley" of Clemson's home turf, a stadium filled with a sea of 81,500 spectators. Amidst this crowd, two tiny groups of Marshall fans stand at opposite ends. Then, from one end, like the soft hum of a beginning storm, the chant begins, "We are..." The response from the opposite end? "Marshall!" The voices weren't many, but the pride was mountainous. By the way, the Herd won 13-10.

For Robert, "We are... Marshall" is much more than a chant. It's a reminder of an unforgettable time, a reminder of his enduring passion for Thundering Herd football.

Lingering Mysteries

Have there ever been any reports of paranormal activity at the Marshall plane crash site? The question was posted in the Huntington, WVa. forum of the Topix.com website.

You may or may not believe in the existence of the paranormal. Even so, the forum has some thought-provoking comments. A former airport employee – "A Witness" of Scott Depot, WVa. – shared this recollection on the forum in October 2010:

"Must have been 20 or so years back as far as I can remember. I was mowing the grass around the Tri-State Airport when I heard a loud roar and saw a large passenger jet slam into the hillside over the edge of where I was working.

I thought I had lost my mind. But instinctively, I ran toward the site where I saw the plane crash. What did I find when I finally made it to what I later found out was the exact spot where the Marshall flight crashed?

Nothing.

It wasn't what I saw, but what I heard that sent shivers down my spine. I heard a faint chant, as if the 75 passengers of the doomed flight were speaking in unison, 'we are, Marshall, we are, Marshall.' I didn't bother telling anyone for some time as I knew I would be labeled 'psychotic.'

To this day I know what I heard and no one will ever tell me otherwise. I always felt a presence in the air while I worked at the airport and that day was just far more bizarre than usual. People don't appreciate the great number of lives lost in the immediate area surrounding the airport. There's bound to be a lot of paranormal activity there."

"A Witness" isn't the only person who weighed in on this topic. On this same Topix.com forum, "I Know" of South Point, Ohio wrote:

"There were some very strange occurrences that happened on campus while the crew for *We Are Marshall* was filming ... especially during the filming of the fountain scene. I was there.

The almost palpable presence of 'something' is always there at the ceremony when MU celebrates the anniversary of the crash."

CHAPTER FIFTEEN

Never Truly Gone

Within the close-knit black student community at Marshall, a profound silence settled over us. Although there was a strong cultural connection, it would be a stretch to say we were all "bosom buddies." The plane crash wasn't just mind-blowing—it was a bone-chilling reality that sent shivers down our spines. It's one thing to feel a collective heartbreak, but it's another to voice it. It felt like we'd returned from a battlefield; you know, how soldiers, despite the chaos they've witnessed, often shield their tales of the warfront? Our hush about that dreadful November night was eerily similar. Why, you ask? To be honest, it's still a mystery.

Maybe we struggled to find words for our deep-seated pain. Or perhaps, we instinctively clung to silence, seeing it as the easiest way to deal with our grief. Emotions are tricky, and trying to explain those feelings is like trying to hold water in your hand. Bill Redd, a fellow student, captured it perfectly: "The crash left an emptiness we couldn't ignore, yet couldn't confront. That agony, trapped inside, kept gnawing at us. Honestly, we should've shouted, cried, or simply talked. Anything to let it all out."

Janice Cooley, haunted by memories for what felt like forever, was weighed down by the pain of losing her boyfriend, Art Harris. But her sorrow was more than just personal. She saw the shadows of grief in the eyes of countless others. Even years later, mentioning that tragedy brings tears to her eyes. "It's still a sensitive subject for me," she admits. "I always looked at it (personal feelings) as something that's very private.

When I was first approached (about sharing my thoughts for a book), I was reluctant. Then I thought: *this is something I need to do.*"

Reaching out to former Marshall schoolmates, the depth of our collective silence struck me like a thunderbolt. Sure, we all lived through that horrific period, but decades later, I was stunned to uncover stories, raw and unspoken, from my peers. Every conversation was a revelation, often making me exclaim, *"Why have I never known this before?"* These untold tales painted a broad spectrum of our shared history, diving deep into personal battles long after the plane crash headlines faded. Looking back, it could be that our silence was a symptom of the times.

In a world unprepared for candid discussions about grief, the comfort offered by modern grief counseling seemed like a far-off dream. Unlike the robust support systems established after the tragic events at Columbine High School and Virginia Tech University, we had nothing. Maybe, just maybe, that's why many of us chose to selectively block out specifics of events associated with the plane crash. Blocking out served as a sedative of sorts to numb the heartache and find some semblance of peace.

Imagine being a vibrant cheerleader one day, and the next, grappling with a nightmarish reality that shatters your world. That's exactly what happened to Debbie (Bailey) Bowen. On the night of the tragedy, Debbie began burying her memories, as if hiding them deep within could make the pain go away. "Surely, it must be some other plane," she hoped, after hearing the first reports about the MU plane going down. But the grim truth stared back at her when she saw Joe Hood's ring, a stark reminder of the fiery tragedy. To make matters worse, she was asked to visit the makeshift morgue to help identify Hood.

"Immediately I said absolutely not," she declared. The very idea of seeing the charred remains did not sit well with Debbie. "Why would I want to subject myself to that?," she argued. And besides, how could she face the reality of what had happened to Joe? After the funerals, as she roamed the halls of her school, confusion clouded her every thought, like a thick fog refusing to lift.

Decades later, the silence surrounding the disaster is finally being broken. Perhaps the years have dulled the sharp edges of pain. Or, maybe folks have grown tired of carrying the heavy baggage of being tight-lipped for so long. For many, the crash became an unspeakable memory, and that includes me, a guy who once shared the field with many of the players who perished. When I walked away from the game, there was a disconnect. Wasn't on the team in '70. Wasn't on the team in '71, so I never felt the need to talk to anyone.

It was a few years after the crash before Marshall experienced any sense of normalcy. Yet, it's debatable as to when that actually happened. Gina (Starling) Gunn argues it was only after her freshman class of '70 had turned their tassels and thrown their graduation caps into the air. "The only time I remember any real conversation taking place about the crash was around time for the anniversary," Gina recalls. "After that day, it was like it was brushed aside." With the graduation of Gina's class, the direct, personal connection to the tragic '70 team faded. Subsequent students heard tales and whispered accounts, but they couldn't grasp the raw, visceral emotions that had enveloped the campus like a dark cloud.

Today, many still wrestle with understanding the depth of grief that held the college and city captive. For those who lived through it, that night remains an indelible scar, a haunting reminder of a tragedy that changed lives forever. Even now, it's still difficult for those of us who were left behind to fully comprehend it all.

With distance and time, memories of the past have a way of echoing into our present lives. It's a phenomenon Janice Cooley encountered in an unexpected place: a business meeting on the West Coast. The subject of the Marshall disaster came up in the conversation. Many around the table were aware of Janice's personal connection to the tragedy, an association that normally formed a tacit, unbreached boundary of discussion. In this instance, however, one of her colleagues ventured into this previously unchartered territory and posed a question about a touchy subject.

"How do you ever get over something like that?"

The question was charged with empathy, piercing through the typical professional decorum. Janice truly appreciated her colleague's genuine concern, so it was OK. She drew in a deep breath, gathering her thoughts when, in an unexpected turn, the same colleague provided the answer she was about to utter.

"You don't. You don't."

Janice was taken aback. The compassion and understanding in her colleague's response had brought her an unexpected sense of comfort. "She was exactly right," Janice admitted. "I just wanted to hug her and tell her that."

The semester following the crash was especially difficult. The intensity of bereavement on campus during the spring of '71 wasn't much different from the night the Marshall plane went down. This proved to be a make-or-break time when people made decisions about their college futures. Most opted to remain at MU; others felt they would best be served by a change of scenery. For those who eventually transferred to other schools, the familiar sights around campus and around the city brought back too many heartbreaking memories of the players who died.

Angela Dodson recalls a conversation she overheard between two coeds on her dorm floor. One of the ladies, a girlfriend of one of the deceased players, bared her soul to a friend about her daily struggles in coping with her loss.

"Are you sure that leaving here is what you really want to do?," the first woman softly inquired.

"It's hard for me to go through this every day," responded the grief-stricken girlfriend, her voice barely above a whisper.

"What's going on?," the first woman probed gently.

"Everywhere I go, I keep looking for him," the teary-eyed woman confessed. "Every time I turn a corner, I just know that we'll run into each other."

The first woman, pausing to gather her thoughts, attempted to provide some comfort. "In time, things could get better, you know."

The other woman shook her head slowly. "If I stay here, I know that what I'm dealing with now, will continue to happen. But if I'm on another campus, I won't have to worry about that. That's why I know it's best for me to go." She paused, her gaze distant as if lost in a memory.

Speaking of memories, every time I think of the crash, the songs from that era come rushing back. Specifically, "Fire and Rain" by James Taylor and "One Less Bell to Answer" by The 5th Dimension. Those songs, for many of us, encapsulate the emotional turmoil of losing a loved one in that tragedy. Music, you know, has a way of piercing the heart, invoking memories that lie deep within, some treasured and others best forgotten.

Flashback to a few months after the crash. Picture this: a dimly lit off-campus apartment living room, with the clock hands inching towards the wee hours. Soft tunes floated in the air, filling the space with a sense of nostalgia. But when the opening notes of "One Less Bell to Answer" wafted through, my mind was instantly transported to that cold November night. The very thought of those girlfriends, mourning their lost boyfriends, plunged me into a sea of sorrow.

"One Less Bell ..." paints the picture of a woman torn apart by heartbreak, and I often wondered, why on earth would someone queue that up at a party? Especially a party at Marshall, and so soon after the crash. It's hardly the kind of tune to spark romance. Yet, as the lyrics unfurled, the connection between them and that dreadful night became undeniably clear. The line—"One less man to pick up after"—felt like a dagger to my heart. The weight of sorrow pressed down on me, and my thoughts turned to Janice Cooley, Macie Lugo, and others, navigating the treacherous waters of grief. How were they coping with the void left by their beloved beaus?

Just as we grapple with the absences in our lives, so too does the unsettling void at a closed casket funeral. It's like a book missing its last chapter, where the main character is absent from the final pages. The desire to see, to touch, to say one last goodbye is rooted deep within us. It's human nature, our way of making sense of the profound mystery of death. But what if that final curtain call is taken away from us? All that remained for the families of the Marshall plane crash victims was a framed photo, which served as a lasting reminder of their loved ones. No final touch, no final look. Simply a picture.

You may wonder why that last touch, that last look, matters so much. Think of the human connections we forge every day—a mother's caress, a friend's pat on the back, a lover's embrace. They're essential in grasping our shared human connection. And in the realm of understanding such profound connections, particularly amidst loss, there are voices that guide us through.

In the turbulent waters of heartache, Gary Young emerges as a pillar of wisdom. Here's a man who, along with his wife Kathy, brought the world *Loss and Found* (2006)—a guide for souls left behind after the untimely death of a spouse at a young age. This work serves as a North star in the wilderness of sorrow. Gary's voice is a testament to the importance of sharing our pain, of bridging that chasm of loneliness and loss. He believes, "It's never too late to heal," a sentiment that deeply resonates.

Similarly, on a broader scale, historic tragedies continue to impact communities. For many, the Marshall plane crash has faded into the pages of history. But for those touched by the tragedy, it remains as indelible as a scar, a perpetual reminder of loss. The Homegoing Caravan might have provided closure for some, but healing is a journey, not a destination. And so, when journeying into the past and visiting the Spring Hill Cemetery memorial—what emerges is more than mere nostalgia. It's a reconnection, a deep dive into a pool of emotions, some painful, some hopeful.

Atop the hill, the memorial stands as a sweeping vista of memories that unfolds before the eyes. From this vantage point, the Twin Towers dormitory rises into view, its backdrop once filled by football fields now absent. Here, six anonymous grave markers echo the mystery of players who couldn't be identified. Yet, among the engraved names on the granite cenotaph, there's a sense of everlasting youth—a team forever frozen in their prime. Visiting this hill is an experience, a mingling of sorrow and peace. A chance to revisit a chapter of one's life, turning the pages with reverence. It's a testament to the power of places, and the emotions they cradle within their borders. And while this memorial at Spring Hill speaks to a universal remembrance, for a specific group at Marshall, the bond runs even deeper and resonates uniquely.

Marshall's black students of the late '60s and early '70s share a bond forged in the crucible of collective sorrow. It's a bond that goes beyond shared classes or campus memories. We were united by a tragedy, our roots intertwined in grief and resilience. And with the passage of time, as Marshall celebrated football triumphs, our hearts swelled with pride. We remembered the past, the pain, and the phoenix-like rise of the Thundering Herd.

Today, as senior citizens, we might look back and marvel at the journey we've taken. From witnessing a tragic crash to seeing our beloved football team rise from the ashes. From youthful days on the campus to the joys and inevitable heartaches of life. But in the autumn of our lives, as November 14th approaches, our hearts beat in unison, remembering the '70 team, and the lasting mark they left behind. For me personally, the Marshall plane crash is an etching of sorrow and strength that time cannot blur. Its memory lingers and still shapes thoughts and perspectives. Erasing it? Impossible, and why would I want to? Those haunting images, stories of resilience, they're part of who I am.

But whoaaa! Hold onto your seats, ladies and gentlemen, for I have an eyebrow-raising revelation to share. Despite my connection to Thundering Herd football, I *deliberately* sidestepped the annual fountain ceremony. In the tapestry of my memories, that ceremony always stood as a poignant reminder of that one horrific night when Marshall's plane went down. Delving into that despair was not my cup of tea. My ties to the tragedy run deep; faces of the guys I played with, voices in memory. I was there when the pain was raw, tears fell, skies darkened. Lived through it, carried their stories. I've walked the path of grief and recovery, not just from books, but from experience.

The aftermath of the crash is not past tense. It's a living reminder of strength and compassion. This matters because to forget, is to forsake the lives lost and lessons learned. *After all this time*, it still matters. And it always will.

Whenever I hear any mention of the Marshall tragedy, a mind-numbing thought hounds me to the hilt. My life could have ended on a chilly November night over 50 years ago on a muddy hillside in West Virginia. It's so clear to me now that God had another plan.

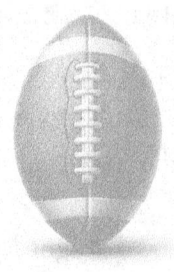

CHAPTER SIXTEEN

Captivating Insights: a Keynote Revelation

As I stood on the podium during the 2023 Fountain Ceremony at Marshall University, the atmosphere of the moment was electrifying. Being the keynote speaker to honor the memories of those who perished in the 1970 plane crash, filled me with a sense of heartfelt responsibility. Previously, I had never attended this annual ceremony, my perception clouded by the sorrow and grief of the tragedy.

But what I had learned, and what I was there to share, was that there's so much more to the Marshall story than the night of the crash. There are other chapters that deserve their time on center stage. That's why I accepted the invitation to speak, eager to unveil aspects of this story that most people knew little or nothing about. My role transcended mere storytelling; it was all about giving voice to the silent whispers of history.

As I surveyed the crowd, I was overjoyed, yet humbled, to be part of this solemn occasion. Every word I chose was designed to resonate deeply, not just with the minds, but with the hearts of everyone present. I wanted the audience, and now my readers, to feel what it was like to be there, to experience the range of emotions that flowed over half-a-century ago. It was a journey through time, inner feelings, and unspoken truths.

What follows is the transcript of my keynote address from start to finish.

Keynote Speech

Today, I'm going to share some unique narratives and perspectives about the Marshall plane crash and its aftermath. For that reason, I encourage you to listen with an open heart and an open mind. Let's pay tribute to the legacy of the 75, not only through our heartfelt remembrance, but by cultivating a deeper understanding of our shared humanity.

You know, it's really an odd feeling for me to be on *this* podium, on *this* day, in *this* environment. For 41 years, I felt a disconnect with Marshall football. Even though I came to Marshall and played with many of the guys who died in the crash, I always felt that I was far removed from November 14, 1970. How come? I was not a member of *that* team. All that changed when I saw the documentary *Ashes to Glory*.

There are some sequences in the documentary that always blow me away. The voice-over talks about the Herd's secondary in '70, and the first name called is No. 21, Felix Jordan, a safety ..... But whoa ... hold on a minute! The picture on the screen *is* No. 21, *but it ain't Felix! It's me!* ... Same jersey number, same position, different year. That's only the beginning. Even more mind-boggling is that *seven times* during the documentary – *seven times* – my image appears when Felix's name is called. How eerie is that?

And here's another strange twist. The case of mistaken identity didn't come to light *until* the documentary's premiere. You'll see my recurring photos in the VCR version, but those were deleted in the DVD release.

Felix Jordan, by the way, was not on the plane. He was removed from the airport-bound bus – *at the last minute* – to accommodate an athletic booster who helped pay for the cost of the flight.

Hmmmm... makes me wonder ... *Maybe* I was a lot closer to Thundering Herd football than I thought.

*****

Now that you have a better understanding about my Marshall connection, I invite you to fasten your seat belt and take a ride with me. Let's go back-back-back in time. The night of the crash was unlike anything I've ever been associated with. There was nowhere you could go to escape the anguish, deep sorrow and the feeling of being totally helpless.

Yet, as a black student back in the day, I could never discuss the night of November 14th, without talking about what transpired the day before, which was Friday the 13th that year.

It all started at an intramural playoff football game between Black United Students and the Kappa Alpha fraternity. The game was intense – on the field and in the stands. The KAs agitated blacks by gleefully waving Confederate flags – an openly brazen display of racial taunting. For us, the flag was and still is symbolic of white supremacy, blatant bigotry and racial hatred.

When the game ended, I watched in amazement as KA pledges ran through groups of black students waving those flags. So, it was hardly surprising that a brawl erupted. Three guys were injured and taken to the hospital.

That was Round one. Round two, which involved two ladies, one black, one white, took place in the Twin Towers cafeteria. At the risk of being too graphic in describing that fight, let's just say it's a good thing that somebody intervened. Otherwise, it would have been one bloody mess. And that's not an exaggeration, folks.

Meanwhile, the Twin Towers lobby on the women's side, was packed to the brim with a shoulder-to-shoulder crowd. Whites on one side, blacks on the other side. You don't know at that point what's going to happen. Who's going to make the first move? Who's going to back down? Who's going to flinch? Who's going to say something wrong? All these things are going on.

Suddenly, one of the football players muscles his way in-between the two groups and demands that they shut it down. Larry "the Governor" Brown made it known that any punches thrown would have to come through him. The mood was still tense, but had toned down just a tick or two as the city police arrived at the scene. Not long after the police arrived, the crowd dispersed.

However, that was not the end of that episode. There was an unsettling uneasiness among black students. Rumors quickly spread that the KAs had reached out to frat brothers from other campuses, urging them to come to Marshall and "settle some scores." So, the word went out among us to stay in a group and not go anywhere by yourself. Not only for that night, but for the entire weekend.

You gotta understand that from the perspective of a black student from back in the day, there was anger. There was fear. There was apprehension. And there was the scary realization that you might be forced to defend yourself ... *by any means necessary.* A lot of us were on edge. And even now, to this very day, I remain fully convinced that we were on the verge of a full-scale race riot on Marshall's campus. I want you to let that sink in for a minute.

Now ... let's push the clock forward another 27-28 hours and now you're dealing with the plane crash and the immediate shockwaves that touched every heart and every mind. The gravity of grief is overwhelming. At that point, we're not thinking about the n-word. We're not thinking about racial bickering. We're not thinking about rebel flags. *It was as if the Friday the 13th fights had never happened.*

Ladies and gentlemen, this was not a black thing. This was not a white thing. This was a death thing and death does not discriminate. So, in ways that perhaps no one would ever have imagined, the football team from' 70, really served as agents of peace between the races.

There's another part to that story that's never been told as far as I know. During the spring of '71, there were 10 black students who were brought up on charges by the Student Court. They were charged with assault. If they were to be convicted, they would be expelled from school.

The situation from the black perspective looked bleak because there was only one member of the Student Court (Bill Redd, a good friend of mine who passed away a couple of summers ago), who would not be biased in rendering a verdict. But what happened when the court examined the evidence, what they found was this was not a situation of random violence, but of provocation. As a result, the charges were dropped and nobody got kicked out of school.

*****

Now, let's backtrack to (the days) right after the crash. At that point, the emphasis was about what to do about these funerals. With so many deaths, there were questions. Where do you go? When do you go? How will you get there?

Here's where the Homegoing Caravan comes into play. The Caravan took on a crucial role, serving as a means to *guarantee* a strong presence of Marshall's black students at the funeral services held for each of the ten black players who died. This was *our way* of paying *our respects. Our way* of standing in solidarity. *Our way* of commemorating their lives as a united community.

Thanks to generous donations and masterful planning by Rev. Charles Smith, the project came together in a matter of days. Some of us traveled by jet to Texas (for funerals in Dallas and Waco). Others drove by car to New Jersey. Most of the rest (58 students) went on a chartered bus trip that made stops in Bluefield, West Virginia, Atlanta, Tuscaloosa, Alabama and Greenwood, South Carolina. This was a tearful, tearful, tearful trek. It covered 1,500 miles in about 4 ½ days.

If you're on that bus, imagine what it must have felt like to go through all those emotional ups and downs ... going from one funeral to the next. There's an interesting note about the first day of the trip.

Given the long ride from Bluefield to Atlanta, the group didn't reach its destination until around 11:30 that night. Fortunately, prior arrangements had been made and the funeral home stayed open so that the group could attend the wake of Larry "the Governor" Brown. They stayed about 40 minutes, and some people might say that was disrespectful. Well, not in this case. The short visit was not a slight to Larry Brown's family. It was necessary because of an extremely tight schedule.

That bus had to be in Tuscaloosa the next day for the joint funeral of four guys from the same hometown who graduated from the same high school. The joint service was gut-wrenching and downright emotionally draining, and that's putting it mildly. After an overnight stay in Tuscaloosa at Stillman College, and a down-home Sunday morning southern breakfast, the group got back on the road and headed east to South Carolina for the final stop.

Now you may ask, why so much focus on the black players? Given the totality of the tragedy, how do you explain this? It's a fair question. To get some perspective, let's put things in the proper context. The '70s were a unique time in American history. The civil rights movement of the '60s had made significant strides. However, racial turmoil was still widespread. Colleges and universities, *including Marshall*, were microcosms of this broader social landscape.

Black students were allowed to go to these mainstream schools, but acceptance was an ongoing journey. In other words, there's a distinct difference between being tolerated and genuine acceptance.

Back then, Marshall had about 300 blacks within a student body of about 7,500. To lose all 10 of us at once in such horrific fashion was devastating. This was personal to us. This was personal! These individuals were more than some dudes who played ball. They were our brothers. We shared a profound bond, rooted in our collective history of fighting for equality. Our mutual heritage and our joint aspirations for a brighter future brought us even closer together.

Perhaps this explains why there was such a gnawing need to pay tribute, to spend time with family members of our fallen brothers. As we pay homage to the 75 souls that were lost, let's also appreciate the tapestries within the tapestry, the stories within the story. Let's recognize that in understanding the unique journeys of each community, we draw closer as one human family.

The "Homegoing Caravan" was not a departure from unity, but rather a deep dive into the beauty of individual stories that make our collective narrative that much richer.

*****

It's important to recognize that tragedies can have a long-term impact. Need proof? Consider the story of Janice Cooley, who dated Art Harris, a star running back. Janice was one of many coeds who endured immense sorrow and pain in losing someone dear in the crash.

In an interview, Janice opened up about her experience, and shared this touching memory with me.

The year is 2004 (keep that year in mind), and Janice, a human resources professional, is conducting a job interview. She scans the applicant's resume and notes that he graduated from the University of Virginia. She mentions that she's from West Virginia and graduated from Marshall.

Here's where things get super intriguing. The applicant reveals that he considered coming to Marshall. Not only that, but his best friend in high school was actually at Marshall and was on the plane with the 75. So now, Janice is eager for an answer, "Well, who was your best friend?" The guy paused a little bit and said .... Art Harris.

Janice was stunned. These were strangers who had a common bond that neither knew they had prior to the interview. She found out that the applicant knew *everything* about Art's family and he knew *everything* about Art. How's that for lasting impact? ... *Thirty-four years after the fact!*

*****

Given that so much time has passed since the tragedy, the question always comes up. Why continue to acknowledge this year after year after year? Yes, the sorrowful part is very hard, very difficult to deal with. But it's not the only aspect. Things come full circle when you consider the big picture.

What happened after the tragedy? How did things turn out because folks decided to keep pressing on instead of folding their tents and calling it a day? When you look at the results, that's the undeniable evidence that good things can and do happen in the wake of awful circumstances. Most folks might describe this as resilience. I call it bounce-back-ability.

The seeds for today's success were sown many years ago. And we're the beneficiaries, so let's keep telling the story, so that it remains fresh in the minds of every generation. It's a timeless story, a story that's worth telling.

*****

When it comes to the crash and its aftermath, there are so many critical lessons to be learned. Tenacity, resolve, the power of community, perseverance, etc.. In this instance, let me hone in on one lesson …. If there's something that you truly want to accomplish, you must keep going. Don't stop. You don't give up and you don't give in … Ever.

The '70 team is a prime example. Really? The Herd (3-6) wasn't even a .500 team. So, what am I talking about? I'm talking about looking beyond the obvious. I'm talking about taking a peek beneath the surface. And in this instance, what you'll find is that in four of those six losses, the average margin of defeat was 3 ½ points. So, it's very feasible that the '70 Herd could have been 7-2 after the East Carolina game.

So, what's the point? My point is this. *The '70 team was not that far off the mark.* The same might be said for your situation, whatever that might be. You keep going because you have no idea how close you are to achieving your goal, to making that dream come true. This is a principle that applies to every endeavor. If you stop, you'll never know the final outcome, and that would be a crying shame. This applies to everything you can think of, not just football. It was valid back in the day, it's valid now, and will still be valid as the years roll on.

*****

On a personal note, I have to admit, this has been quite a journey, a long and winding road full of surprises and sometimes startling revelations. Whenever I hear mention of the Marshall plane crash, there's always a mind-numbing thought that crops up …. My life could have ended over 50 years ago on a muddy hillside in West Virginia. It's so clear to me now that God had another plan.

God has a plan for all of us. If you haven't given your life to Him, the time to surrender is now. It's never a foolish idea to have a talk with our Creator. The Bible makes this extremely clear in II Chronicles… "If my people, which are called by my name, will humble themselves, and pray, and seek my face, and turn from their wicked ways, then will I hear from heaven, and will forgive their sin, and will heal their land." Be blessed on this day and always, for there is nothing that can separate you from the love of God.

This is Craig T. Greenlee, I'm from Jacksonville, F-L-A, and I thank you for listening.

Keynote speaker Craig T. Greenlee deeply engages the audience at the 2023 Fountain Ceremony, honoring the 1970 plane crash victims and shedding light on untold aspects of the tragedy and its aftermath. (Photo courtesy of Marshall University)

As the sun shines down on an unseasonably warm November day, the audience at the Fountain Ceremony stands absorbed and welcoming. (Photo courtesy of Marshall University)

Herd lineman Dalton Tucker, who has the same jersey number
once worn by Larry "the Governor " Brown, a crash victim, offers
a rose in remembrance. This touching gesture symbolizes their
intertwined histories. (Photo courtesy of Marshall University)

APPENDIX

Memories of Marshall
By John Kiesewetter
Cincinnati Enquirer
December 24, 2006

Printed with permission from *The Enquirer*

Felix Jordan, who might have been on the fateful plane ride, thinks each day of the friends he lost.

Felix Jordan doesn't need to see the new *We Are Marshall* movie to understand the horror of the Marshall University football team perishing in a 1970 plane crash. "I know I'm going to think about it when I open my eyes up every day," says Jordan, 55, one of three Marshall varsity players who didn't make that fateful trip to East Carolina University.

"There's not a day that goes by that I don't think about it," says Jordan, a 1969 Sycamore High School graduate who missed the game as a sophomore because he had a severely sprained ankle and was asked by his coach to give up his seat to a team booster.

"I have dreams about my teammates. I have flashbacks, like they're right there next to me. Sometimes I find myself talking to somebody (who died)," says Jordan in his first interview about the crash since the movie project began nearly two years ago. It opened nationwide Friday.

Jordan was hanging out with friends in a Marshall cafeteria in Huntington, W.Va., when they heard about the crash at nearby Tri-State Airport on Nov. 14, 1970. Jordan, freshman quarterback Reggie Oliver and several athletes immediately drove to the crash scene. "We came over this hill and could just see the side of the mountain burning," says Jordan, now a maintenance employee at the Blue Ash Clarion Hotel & Suites. He returned to the wreckage the next day to help recover teammates' bodies.

In the year of the 50th anniversary of the plane crash, the Marshall campus was adorned with banners featuring the faces of the 75 individuals who lost their lives. (Photo by Vic Simpson)

In all, 75 people died in the crash, including the head coach and most of his assistants; three Moeller High School graduates on the team—Bob Harris, Jack Repasy and Mark Andrews; trainer Jim Schroer, a McNicholas High School graduate; and boosters.

"It was still smoking the next day when we went out to help. There wasn't much there to identify the bodies. I threw up. I couldn't do it."

But you won't see Jordan in the film.

He and teammate Ed Carter, now a Tennessee minister, did not grant Warner Bros. rights to use their likenesses. So screenwriter Jamie Linden tells the story of rebuilding the football team through defensive back Nate Ruffin (Anthony Mackie)—the third player who stayed behind—plus new coach Jack Lengyel (Matthew McConaughey), assistant coach Red Dawson (Matthew Fox) and Oliver (Arlen Escarpeta).

"Nobody was able to reach him (Jordan)," Linden says in a phone interview from Los Angeles.

Jordan says he received a letter from Warner Bros. and called the Los Angeles numbers as requested, but never spoke to anyone about the film. "If they had reached me, I would have talked to them—but I probably wouldn't have signed my rights away," he says. "My friends are more upset about me not being in the movie than I am."

The film, which Jordan saw at a recent preview, depicts the two other returning players as a chubby African-American with an ankle cast and crutches, and a short white player. "We had to change distinct characteristics," Linden says.

Jordan admits he had reservations about recounting the excruciating details for a Hollywood writer.

Life has not been easy for him. He walks with a limp from falling off a ladder. He has bad knees from playing on Marshall's rock-hard artificial turf field. Although he earned a history degree at Marshall and thought of becoming a teacher, Jordan ended up in Detroit installing phone and cable TV systems. Since returning here about 10 years ago, he has worked mostly in motel maintenance.

Jordan, whose younger brother Paul was a Parade All-American running back at Sycamore in 1972, also admits he had used alcohol and drugs to ease his emotional and physical pain. "When something like this happens now, (grief) counselors come to the school. All we had was a Catholic priest to talk to. And he was the team chaplain, and he was as torn up as we were," Jordan says. "They hadn't even come up with the term 'post traumatic stress.' So you had to John Wayne your way through it. Real men don't cry, and all that. But I cried like a baby.

"People can't understand what you're going through. I tell them: What if you lost 35-40 members of your immediate family, just like that? That's basically what happened. One day they were all there, and the next they were all gone. I get depressed thinking about it. Why did I live? I still don't know the reason 36 years later."

Although he couldn't play, Jordan was scheduled to fly with the team to Greenville. Hours before departure, assistant coach Frank Loria told Jordan he would stay home because his seat on the chartered DC-9 was needed for a former Marshall boosters president. (That is not depicted in the movie.)

Watching the film, Jordan saw his No. 21 jersey on a player during the re-enactment of the 1971 Marshall-Xavier University game. He says he's not surprised that Ruffin, who died in 2001, gets credit for things Jordan says he did, such as calling defensive signals on the field. The film is "about 40 percent accurate," he says. "That's Hollywood. I know they had to make it entertaining," he says. "It was good (not to focus on me) because I'm just naturally introverted. To me, the real heroes were the 75 people in that plane crash."

Bottom line, he's pleased with the production.

"It made Marshall look good, and it didn't make me as sad as I thought," he says. "But most people will go home after the film and can think of something else—but I carry it with me every day."

www.ingramcontent.com/pod-product-compliance
Lightning Source LLC
Chambersburg PA
CBHW071323120626
46546CB00002B/410